VOL. V, No. 2

/81

THE JOURNAL OF PASTORAL PRACTICE

JAY E. ADAMS
Editor-in-Chief

PRESBYTERIAN AND REFORMED PUBLISHING CO.
PHILLIPSBURG, NEW JERSEY

ISBN: 0-87552-036-7

CONTENTS

Continued on next page

CONTENTS *(Continued)*

A Reminder on Suicide

Twelve years ago, when I wrote *Competent to Counsel*, I made a few comments on suicide. Here is what I wrote:

> One of the first things that clients need is hope. Since much despair stems from the general failure of counseling, many people come with little hope. Counselors, therefore, must learn to engender hope by taking people seriously about their sin. For example, if a client says (perhaps almost parenthetically), "I guess I haven't been much of a mother or wife," she probably expects the counselor to minimize her evaluation of herself. Most other people have failed to take her comments seriously in the past. They invariably say something like this: "Don't talk like that Susie; you know you haven't been that bad." Such responses destroy hope, because the client has not been taken seriously. Minimizing responses indicates to the client that the counselor is not going to deal with the problem at the level on which the client believes the problem exists. Hope of help from him is thereby largely diminished. Moreover, minimizing another's adverse evaluation of himself is really a backhanded compliment, because while it wrongly tends to excuse bad conduct which the client already recognizes to be bad, and about which he already feels guilty, minimizing further degrades him by telling him he doesn't even know what he is talking about. Minimize a man's estimate of himself and you minimize the man himself.

Nouthetic counselors try not to let the client's adverse evaluations of himself go by without comment, and try never to respond in ways which might minimize the client's bad opinion of himself.[1] Instead, any statement of that sort by a client is promptly investigated. If a client says, "I haven't been a good mother," nouthetic counselors might reply, "That's a serious matter. Tell me about it. What have you been doing? How have you been failing as a mother?" If she says, "I have not been much of a wife," they might say, "Well, now, that's a serious matter before God; how have you failed as a wife?"

When counselors take clients seriously, they usually respond quickly, pouring out problems, failures and sins. Others who minimize such

---

1. In suicidal cases, when a client has such a low opinion of himself that he thinks the world would be better off without him, it only hurts to deny that his low estimate is valid. Counselors should acknowledge that he is probably right about the present worthlessness of his life, and should attempt to discover how bad he has been. However, they should take issue with his proposed solution, and instead point him to God's solution through repentance and holy living.

comments frequently succeed only in pushing material back down inside the client again. Clients understandably do not want to reveal themselves to someone who won't take them seriously. Many clients receive some help almost immediately from the fact that someone at last has taken them seriously. Taking people seriously about their sins is an important way to give them hope.

Christ's consistent approach toward those who came to him was to take their sins into account. His characteristic phrase was, "Your sins have been forgiven you." Far from minimizing sins, he often raised the issue of sin with those who themselves failed to do so. Cf. the story of the Rich Young Ruler (Luke 18:18-23).[2]

Now, today, as I opened my newspaper, I read:

"Mayor Said He Was Going to Kill Himself"

ANNAPOLIS, MD. (AP)—Members of the City Council say they didn't believe acting Mayor Gustav J. Akerland when he told them he was so worried about the city's fiscal problems that he was going to shoot himself.

The 60-year-old Akerland died Wednesday at Anne Arundel General Hospital where he had been since Saturday after shooting himself in the head.

Several days before the shooting, Akerland told city council colleagues he had some good news for them.

"The good news is that in 11 hours I'm going to shoot myself," said Akerland.

"We all said: 'Come on Gus, it's not that bad, don't let it get you down,' " Alderman David O. Colburn recalled Wednesday. "We had no idea he was serious."

Police found Akerland when they responded to a silent alarm in the municipal building.

Police investigators found five documents in Akerland's office, including a two-page memorandum in which the acting mayor despaired over his inability to complete the 1982 budget before an April 30 deadline.[3]

Note especially Alderman Colburn's words: "Come on, Gus, it's not all that bad"—that is minimizing of the first order! Note also the words: "We had no idea he was serious." No idea he was *serious*—they did not take him seriously when he announced his plan. Always take a person seriously when he makes self-accusations. Here is a startling example of what I have been trying to get across for some time. Read this account and note the *very elements* that I have warned you to avoid.—J.E.A.

---

2. *Competent to Counsel* (Phillipsburg, N.J.: Presbyterian and Reformed, 1970), pp. 140-41.

3. *Macon Telegraph,* April 17, 1981, p. 4B.

Counseling

HOWARD A. EYRICH
Editor

Howard A. Eyrich is a counselor in the CCEF offices in Atlanta and Macon, Georgia. He holds the Th.M. from Dallas Theological Seminary and the D.Min. from Western Conservative Baptist Seminary in Portland, Oregon.

"LIFESTYLE THERAPY"
The New Task for Health Education
TIM CRATER

In a previous essay[1] I attempted to draw further attention to the developing connection between the mental health field and public education. The secular experts who work in the field of behavioral problems and who insist on calling them medical problems are supplying modern educators with their concepts for use in the classrooms on the public's children. Since in society at large the notion of mental illness is being allowed to stand virtually unchallenged, it is actually quite reasonable to expect public educators to incorporate its nostrums into the classroom, since historically the schools have been greatly involved in true (physical) health matters relating to children. Consequently, we should not be surprised to find that one of the major conduits through which secular religious views are being passed on to children in the public classroom is the area of "health education," which has now been expanded to include "mental" health.

A recent textbook published for use in public education exemplifies this trend toward mental health education. The title is *Toward a Healthy Lifestyle Through Elementary Health Education* ("With an Atlas of Instructional Materials"), published by Wadsworth Publishing Co., Belmont, California. The authors are John J. Burt of the University of Maryland, Linda Brower Meeks of Ohio State, and Sharon Mitchell Pottebaum of the Ohio Department of Health. The direction this book takes is clearly suggested in the title; we are going to explore "lifestyles" which, in the judgment of the authors (a qualification they do not make) are "healthy." Not "reasonable," "right," or "wise," but "healthy." Naturally this idea hitchhikes on the reality that with the physical body there is a clear standard, described by science, against which the body should be measured to determine its health or lack thereof. In the authors' view there is a clear standard of health for a lifestyle against which the lives, beliefs, attitudes, and choices of the public's children may be measured. The authors would most likely insist that, as with the body, where true science has

---

1. Tim Crater, "Counselors in the Classroom," *Journal of Pastoral Practice* IV, 2 (1980): 21-30.

described a physical standard, so also with behavior the science of mental health has determined the norm against which the students should be judged and treated for "health."

Now we evangelicals obviously believe there is a norm against which behavior should be judged, and the Bible describes that norm. Our objection is that humanists either do not recognize or seek to conceal that their norm is also a religious norm. Their norm has been cloaked in science and embroidered with the illusion of neutrality and objectivity. Furthermore, our position is frequently assailed as coming from superstition, religious dogma, and irrationality, and is therefore unsuitable material for public education and is not permissible for state sponsored schools. So, while traditional American values are excluded on religious grounds, the state nevertheless is proceeding with religious instruction through values education under the guise of "health" education.

The authors proceed to tell us in their introduction that "advances in science and medicine have resulted in significant changes in the nature of the national health problems" (p. 6). Since science has made major strides against true disease, physical disease, health education must turn its attention to more pressing matters. "The new antagonists," we are informed, "are the conditions that are more susceptible to treatment with changes in lifestyle than to treatment with drugs." Now, not only can your body be treated for illness, but your lifestyle can receive treatment too. And, "to be most effective, the evaluation of lifestyle alternatives should begin in elementary school." Further on they tell us that "although physical problems like tooth decay, malnutrition, and infectious diseases still plague the young, the most pressing problems of youth involve their emotional health, sexuality, safety, drug behavior and overall happiness." These give some idea of what areas of behavior the expanded health education in the schools will attempt to deal with.

To take the sex education area as an example, the authors display the same conception of the school's role as do most modern educators. It takes very little time to explain the basic facts of life, the biological facts of life, where babies come from. It is thus pretty evident that more is contained in the instruction than simple anatomy. The considerable time and effort devoted to this area is explained by the fact that the children are being furnished with a set of values and attitudes to go with the sex education information and it takes time to shape values, as parents and private religious institutions can attest. The authors wish to contribute to the children in this values area as well, and they address the subject in their book in a way that clearly reveals their moral position on certain aspects of sexuality.

Under the heading "Male Growth and Development" (pp. 66f.) they discuss the physical aspects of male sexual development and then turn to the "Search for Sexual Identity," a title obviously suggesting a search for definitive values regarding sex. In their discussion they are quite dogmatic about what information children "should have access to," and what "facts regarding male sexuality should be communicated

6

to all elementary students.'' Apparently, even when one possesses the scientific truth about behavior, one nevertheless must still employ moral terms. They tell us further how children ought to view homosexuality.

> Males may exhibit a sexual orientation in which they are attracted to females, other males, or both. Males who feel sexually attracted toward females are known as heterosexuals. Males who feel attracted toward other males are known as homosexuals. In general, less than 10 percent of all males are homosexual, but the fact that they represent a minority does not mean that they are physically or psychologically abnormal. At the present time, the cause of homosexuality is unknown. Further, an attraction toward persons of the same sex is involuntary. Thus, making fun of homosexuals is a very unkind practice. Given different parents and a different childhood experience, any of us might have developed a different sexual orientation.

Virtually the same words are used later on in connection with female sexuality, adding the concept of "affectional preference" when discussing the homosexual aspect.

A "healthy" lifestyle then *may* include homosexuality; that may turn out to be one's "sexual orientation" or "affectional preference." At the very least it includes a view of homosexuality in which it is not abnormal, is involuntary, and is not considered wrong morally. Though no one talks of looking for the "cause" of heterosexuality (it seems to be a rather natural condition), and though the authors stress that homosexuality has a "cause" as yet undetermined, we must nevertheless teach elementary children that it is merely one among many perfectly acceptable lifestyle options.

Now that kind of assertion doesn't look like a scientific conclusion being passed on dispassionately to inquiring minds; it looks very much like a moral position on a moral issue. Furthermore, what of the admonition against being unkind? Is this a scientific, medical observation? An empirical fact? It looks suspiciously like a moral judgment, the kind of "moralistic preaching" which, if done by one holding traditional moral values, would bring cries of moral outrage from the guardians of the separation of church and state.

Let's be clear here; unkindness to homosexuals is not justifiable. What they do is clearly wrong, but unkindness is not an acceptable response to them from anyone. But what is being communicated here is not that, though *wrong,* homosexuality does not justify cruelty or unkindness. Rather, the children are to be told that homosexuality is an acceptable lifestyle alternative; it is involuntary, and therefore it is not right to make fun or to view it as abnormal.

For all the stress on supposed neutrality of the educational system, we see no neutrality, broadmindedness, or educational freedom being offered elementary children here. They are not presented with a range of views present in our society and asked to pick the one they like. They are given one view; it is merely a sexual preference, and other views, including the one held by generations of educated people in Western civilization, are omitted. Our authors merely state the current secular dogma and expect teacher and student to embrace it uncritically. The effect of this approach must be a child who looks at homosexuality as one possible option which he himself might wish to pursue, as a "healthy" lifestyle alternative.

Here we have a vivid illustration of the thrust of modern education—an attack on traditional moral values with the intent of substituting in their place the values of secular society. Sociologist Alvin Gouldner, in *The Future of Intellectuals and the Rise of the New Class,* observes with approval that through public education, up to and including college, parents unwittingly subsidize the systematic weaning of their children from the values of family and church.[2]

Our authors attribute this new trend in health education, the move toward an emphasis on "mental health," to two basic factors. They say on page 6, under the heading "Resurgence of Humanism," that the "present age may be characterized as predominantly humanistic, for humanistic concepts and values seem to pervade all of contemporary life." Specifically, they say, a renewed concern for "self-actualization" has come along with this resurgence of humanism. They cite Maslow's work in this area and assert that the "concept of self-actualization has a profound effect on priorities in American education. For example today's schools focus much of their attention on personal decision making." Then they proceed to indicate what role health education will play in this humanistic renaissance.

> In this atmosphere of humanism, concern with self-actualization, and personal decision making, health education occupies an important integrating role. That is, much of what is learned in elementary school and many of the decisions that are really secondary to a more important accomplishment: the selection and evaluation of a lifestyle that is healthy and promotes happiness. This latter process is a primary purpose of health education (pp. 6, 7).

Health education, then, will play a vital role, an integrating role whereby the children will put all they learn in elementary experience together and come up with what is called a "healthy lifestyle." Health education will put it all together for them so that they can find the happiest life possible. This will all be done in an admittedly humanistic atmosphere, where humanistic values are pervasive. The tragic thing about this is that they try to maintain on the one hand that they are passing on humanistic values, while on the other that they are being scientific, neutral, and objective. They aren't evangelizing, they believe, or dogmatizing, or sermonizing; they are conveying health information. They are dealing with scientific truth, with mental health which mental health doctors (themselves under the influence of secular humanism) have defined for them. How could any religious parent object? The school isn't dealing with religion, only health education! But as Nobel laureate Milton Friedman observed, the "public schools teach religion, too—not a formal, theistic

2. *National Review Magazine* XXXIII, 3 (Feb. 20, 1980): 139-40.

religion, but a set of values and beliefs that constitute a religion in all but name."[3]

The trend toward mental health education, then, is partially the result of the renewed humanistic concern for "self-actualization." The second factor which our health education book describes is put under the heading, "A Reexamination of the Concept of Mental Health" (p. 7). This is a remarkable section. The authors cite Dr. Thomas Szasz, a well-known opponent of the concept of mental illness, as offering a "new concept" of mental illness. In the quotation from Szasz, he states that the usual definition of psychiatry involves treatment of mental illnesses which he labels "a worthless and misleading definition." He is cited as saying, "Mental illness is a myth. Psychiatrists are not concerned with mental illnesses and their treatments. In actual practice they deal with personal, social, and ethical problems in living." Our authors apparently liked that last part about "ethical problems in living" and seem to have ignored the main thrust of Szasz' comment. He didn't offer a "new concept" of mental health here; he debunked the whole idea and said it was a myth from the start! He was asserting that mental health professionals don't deal with illnesses of the mind; they are dealing with behavior problems—personal, social, and ethical problems in living.

Our authors nevertheless insist that a new concept of mental health has emerged from his words (a beautiful example of eisegesis in a secular setting). They tell us that the result of this new concept with respect to elementary education is the following:

> Spurred on by sociologists and encouraged by humanist ethics, educators began to realize by the 1970s that in actual practice they also dealt with personal, social, and ethical problems in living—that they were, in fact, holding hands with psychiatry. Like psychiatists, teachers also found themselves dealing with matters of sexuality, drug behavior, self-concept, and happiness. Within this new concept of mental health it is currently fashionable for psychiatrists and educators to work together to improve learning.

So while Szasz says get rid of the concept of mental illness and admit that what is involved are behavioral matters, our authors have him saying that not only should the concept of mental illness be retained, but that it should be expanded to *include* ethical problems and moved wholesale into the schools! Now it is one thing to cite Freud, Maslow, or some other modern practitioner of the medical model as one's authority for extending mental health education into the public school classroom, but to extend it under the authority of the secular arch-foe of the very concept of mental illness and health is a remarkable accomplishment indeed. The psychiatrist and teacher may "hold hands" in the public school and all with the blessing of Dr. Szasz.

Under these arrangements not only will the voluntary psychiatric patient (as well as the involuntary patients) enjoy the benefits of humanistic ethics and religion, but now

---

3. Milton and Rose Friedman, *Free to Choose* (New York: Hourcourt, Brace, Jovanovich, 1979), p. 164.

public school children, in compulsory attendance at school, will have the opportunity to go through the humanistic catechism as well. But our authors are careful to point out that this new hand-holding pair will not improve beliefs, ethics, values, and religious ideology, though that is what they will deal with. No, they will work together to "improve learning," and what parent in his right mind could be against that? While ministers with recognized religious ideologies may not hold teachers' hands, psychiatrists with the new humanistic values may romance education to their heart's content, since they are doctors, practitioners of the scientific truth about mental health.

We are seeing in all of this the true nature of those who cite the pluralistic nature of American society as the reason why evangelicals should not impose their views on others, particularly in the public schools. Social reformers, when faced with social activity on the part of evangelicals, have repeatedly cried out that we mustn't seek to "impose" our view (which very often means don't defend it, either). But do they apply the same rule to themselves? As Professor James Hitchcock observed,

> Although the word is often employed as a talisman, there is probably less genuine "pluralism" in America now than two decades ago. As the English historian E. R. Norman has observed, the authority of pluralism is mainly invoked during the period of transition from one orthodoxy to another. Liberal activists now speak of pluralism, or toleration of unpopular ideas, in the context of winning social acceptance of such things as homosexuality and "open marriage." But it is not simply toleration they seek. In reality they believe in a *therapeutic norm in which all are expected to conform* [emphasis mine]. Whatever one's chosen "lifestyle" no one is conceded the right to be a principled moral traditionalist. Much of the influence of the media and the education system is bent toward bleaching out genuine cultural differences (as distinct from picturesque differences) and drawing the entire society within the folds of the liberal moral consensus. . . .[4]

Judging by the trends in society at large and by the related trends in public education, we are truly in a transition (not necessarily an inevitable or irreversible one, however) from a Judeo-Christian consensus to that espoused by liberal activists, and pluralism provides the innovators with a handy key to get their views a hearing, from which vantage point they aim to make them the exclusive orthodoxy. Our textbook is a prime example of their belief in that "therapeutic norm" which everyone must conform to, beginning in the elementary grades. The traditional lifestyle, guided by Judeo-Christian values, is not allowed as a viable option, but is "bleached" out through the process of health education. For all the talk of broad-mindedness and pluralism, there is clearly a new orthodoxy being espoused in public education.

This attempt at the "systematic weaning" (to use Gouldner's term cited above) of

---

4. James Hitchcock, "Is Life a Spectator Sport?," *National Review Magazine* XXXIII, 2 (Feb. 6, 1981): 94-98.

children from the values of family and church certainly ought to concern pastors, Christian counselors, and others in the faith who deal with families with children involved in public education. As a pastor, I have had frequent opportunities to discuss a wide spectrum of problems with the families I minister to, problems which have their origins in the value education efforts of the public schools. How should they respond, for example, to a spiritist coming to the classroom to give a demonstration, or to a required sex education course where the value system which guides the use of sex is not the Christian system? In the midst of writing this I had yet another parent come in to discuss a problem of this sort, a classroom activity in which a non-Christian value system was being conveyed. Pastors ought also to make their people aware that the church and the state schools are increasingly in competition for the values of their children and that they should take a good long look at what is going on in their school under the title "Health Education." The authors of this text seem to relish the possibility of teachers functioning as psychiatrists, and as psychiatrists who espouse a humanistic value system in a humanistic atmosphere. This is a trend that Christian taxpayers (who are helping to subsidize that "weaning process") ought to oppose, whether their own children are in public schools or not, and they ought to do so without apology. It is also a reality which pastors and Christian counselors should be familiar with, as it may well prove to be an influential factor in the behavior of the children whose values we are attempting to shape for Christ.

THE KEY TO THE CASEBOOK

Jay E. Adams

THE JOB HUNTER[1]

"We owe everyone in town, and if Warren doesn't soon get a good job and keep it we may be tarred and feathered and run out of town!" That was the icing that Florence put on the cake. Warren, quite honestly, had detailed a thirteen-year history of failure to make good at supporting his family of three (they had two children—Sally and Rose). Time and again they had been bailed out of financial ruin by Florence's father, but the last time he had put his foot down. "Never again!" he roared. "If you don't make it this time, you can sink!" That was six months ago. At the time everything had looked rosy. Both had become Christians; for a while Warren's new job as head of the shipping department in a large printing firm looked secure, he enjoyed it, and he seemed well suited for the work. But gradually the old problem had returned. Disagreements, complaints, anger, and resentment toward his employer and fellow workers grew until two days ago in a fiery exchange with the plant manager he stormed out of the place and quit. It was then that Florence had insisted upon coming to you for help.

Problems:

1. What problems are apparent?

2. What other problems might possibly be present?

---

1. An expansion on Case no. 4, in J. E. Adams, *The Christian Counselor's Casebook*, (Phillipsburg, N.J.: Presbyterian and Reformed Publishing Co., 1974), pp. 8, 9.

3. Would it be of importance to explore the content of the argument? Why?

4. What patterns may exist?

Homework

In this case, several facts should be noted:
1. Take note of the language of exaggeration, which leads to inexactness, undue emotional arousal, and inability to deal with the problem:
    a. "We owe everyone in town." Ask "How many persons do you actually owe?" and "Exactly how much to each?"
    b. "Tarred and feathered" and "run out of town." Find out precisely—if at all—*which* creditors have been exerting pressure *of what sort,* and *how frequently.*
    c. Point out that such exaggeration distorts truth, and is not the sober, Christian way of dealing with facts.
2. Note how Florence's father has given them a golden opportunity to start afresh on a proper basis.
3. Explore the "old problems" that "had returned." Point out the fact that they had been "put off" (or rather, the attempt had been made—unsuccessfully—to put them off) but there had been no adequate effort to "put on" the alternative biblical patterns that God requires. This attempt to break habits will always be unsuccessful; God insists on *replacing* them by righteous ones (see the *Manual*).
4. Anger seems to be one of the principal problems and must be dealt with. There seems to be a problem with the growing internalization of anger that ultimately explodes. Cf. the *Manual* for more on this. By exploring the content of the argument with the plant manager (a) you may discover what he becomes angry

about (and can show him how God expects him to handle such situations) and (b) you may be able to help him repent of this and return to the manager to seek forgiveness and to request reinstatement.

5. Probably, somewhere along the line, a thorough exploration and application of the Christian work ethic found at the end of Colossians 3 would be necessary.

6. While we know little of Florence, we need to have her present at each session to discover (a) if she contributes to the problem or to its solution, (b) if she can help in the future. Her language makes us suspicious and, at the very least, calls for discussion.

7. The thirteen-year history of failure and dependence indicates the need for repentance, for some basic teaching, coaching and structure. There is much here to investigate and deal with in light of II Thessalonians 3:6-12.

8. There is much hope in this case. Note, especially, Warren's honesty and Florence's insistence on getting help. Evidently, Father's declaration has created a situation in which there is (at last) heavy enough structure to bring about change quickly. Be sure that, at each point where decisions are made, they are done to please God rather than merely to get out of their predicament. The possibility of repaying Father (at least something) when they get on their feet ought to be broached.

Myths of Career Choice

Martin E. Clark

The increasing emphasis on career education in schools and the career development movements in business and industry have combined to create a growing sensitivity to career counseling as a church ministry. Christians correctly understand that God's will for their lives includes His will for their vocations, and so pastors face increasing pressure in helping these decision makers.

In many cases, career decision making is complicated by myths held by the deciders, and perhaps also perpetuated by pastors. One of the first counseling functions in these cases is the replacement of these myths with more genuinely biblical content. Following are several myths which frequently frustrate Christians in making career decisions.

Myth: God's Will Is Mystical

Some have so "spiritualized" God's will that it has become to them a nonrational process. Finding God's will is seen as a crisis experience—probably not a bolt of lightning, but at least something emotionally equivalent to it. The desire for a particular type of experience (usually undefined) prolongs and frustrates the decision process. This myth is complicated by those who advise decision makers that they will "just know it" when they have discovered God's will, or that they should search for a "feeling of peace" as a sign of God's direction.

This myth assumes that God's guidance is essentially different from His daily providential activity in our lives. Consequently, the person operating on this basis neglects to study himself—his abilities, limitations, interests, values, spiritual gifts, etc., which God has placed in his life and is developing on a daily basis. The study of these personal qualities may be profoundly unspectacular, but it is essential in order to know what God has placed in our lives that may have vocational implication. Essentially, a career decision is a stewardship decision, and a steward must know with what he is entrusted before he can exercise proper stewardship.

While God occasionally called persons in Bible times using rather spectacular means involving special revelation (e.g., Isaiah, Paul, Moses), He drastically altered His use of special revelation with the completion of the biblical canon. And even in Bible times, the spectacular was spectacular because it was unusual. The search for a crisis experience as a sign of guidance can be an attempt to escape a healthy, systematic self-examination.

In the same way, some seek a feeling of peace as God's authentication of direction.

Citing Colossians 3:15 ("Let the peace of God rule in your hearts. . . ."), they understand the "peace" to be the critical factor in deciding. The Colossians context, however, does not deal with decision-making, and, more importantly, there is no evidence that "peace" is nonrational in the Christian life. Further, Christians and non-Christians alike experience emotional relief from the process of decision-making itself, and that relief is often interpreted as "peace." Persons seeking peace as a sign usually find it prior to developing very many creative alternatives, thereby cutting short their understanding both of themselves and of the world of work. Once again, instead of seeking a sign, we need to submit to the process of self-examination.

God is orderly. He is neither confused nor the author of our confusion. What He has placed and developed in our lives in the past, and what He is developing in our lives currently, have some relationship to what He wants from our lives in the future. This self-knowledge is required of those entering the pastorate (I Tim. 3; Titus 1), the career decision in which, ironically, the penchant for mysticism is most pronounced. "Feeling called" does not replace fulfilling the criteria explicitly stated in Scripture.

Overcoming the effects of the myth of mysticism usually involves (1) focusing on self-assessment with a great degree of specificity; (2) teaching how to research career opportunities, since such data is relevant and available by common grace and by general revelation; (3) emphasizing commonalities among individual traits and vocational opportunities.

Myth: God's Will Is Unpleasant

How many times have we heard testimonies and messages that focused on "yielding" or "surrendering" to God's will? The message conveyed is that God's will is always opposite to our desires, and that it is something to which we must surrender after a difficult struggle. The terms "surrender" and "yield" further indicate that we are losing, doing God's will only because we were not successful in the struggle. It is assumed that our interests, abilities, and ambitions must be renounced in order to be "in the center of God's will." Some persons, laboring under the added burden of unresolved guilt, may even see God's calling as a punishment.

While it is true that our sin sometimes creates desires that are opposed to God's will, we should not presume that all of our desires and interests are automatically suspect. Psalm 37:4 asserts: "Delight yourself in the Lord; and He will give you the desires of your heart." The believer who is consciously living for Christ ought to expect God to develop his interests and desires to conform to His will. The automatic dichotomy between His will and our will should be challenged, for such division ignores the activity of God in shaping our desires.[1] In fact, Scripture asserts that "if a

---

1. Applying Christ's Gethsemane plea, "Not my will, but Thine be done" (Luke 22:42) to a career decision is a gross distortion of the context. Further, Christ was not surrendering a rebellious will to the Father, but rather, asserting His unity of purpose with the Father.

man aspires to the office of overseer, it is a fine work he desires to do'' (I Tim. 3:1), assuming thereby the presence of personal desire.

Persons laboring under this myth may fear the career decision. Or, they may feel that a route to deeper piety involves choosing what may be most difficult, a self-punishment akin to penance. In either event, the activity of God in developing desires is denied.

Dispelling this myth involves (1) acknowledging God's sovereignty in shaping our desires; (2) developing depth in devotion and worship, so we can affirm that we are delighting in the Lord; (3) handling the unresolved guilt through repentance; (4) developing a biblical philosophy of vocation, in which we acknowledge God's intention for us to find fulfillment in our work.

Myth: God's Will Is Known Once for All Life

Many persons think that they will make only one career decision during life, and once it is made they will never need to rethink their direction. Subsequent confusion causes concern, for these persons often interpret career changes as (1) an admission of a wrong choice earlier, or (2) an evidence of personal instability, or (3) a defection from God's will. Especially those in professional ministry careers experience anguish over career transitions, for our evangelical culture has largely assumed that every call to ministry is a life-time call.

This myth denies the prerogative of God to move in our lives according to His will, to use work experiences to prepare us for later responsibilities, and to reward us for faithfulness. Jesus' parable of the talents clearly indicates that faithfulness at one level of responsibility leads to greater levels of opportunity (Matt. 25:21, 23, 29). When was David in God's will—as a shepherd, a musician, a soldier, a king? No doubt, he was fulfilling the will of God in each case.

If we are genuinely growing, vital believers, our growth will include the discovery and development of new interests, gifts, and goals throughout life. Some of these new factors will necessitate reordering our priorities, and may also point to new ways of exercising stewardship in vocation.

We may have grown up with the phrase, ''Quitters never win,'' and we may apply that to our vocational progress. We think once we have started something, we must pursue it to the bitter end. But quitting is different from changing. Changing involves adapting—to new circumstances, new knowledge of self, newly developed abilities, and/or new priorities. We are new creatures in Christ, and the renewing of our minds is an ongoing process.

One who accepts this myth will feel threatened by career changes, and he may stubbornly persist where he no longer belongs to avoid the fabricated guilt involved in a change. He may fear criticism, and his capacity to decide may be further inhibited by the fear that he made an earlier wrong choice. Dispelling the myth often grants him freedom to explore God's activity in his life in order to respond in more currently faithful stewardship.

Myth: God's Will Is Mysterious

Many Christians are convinced that their career choice will be difficult because God's will can be discovered only with great difficulty. They must search for it, they feel, because He has hidden it. Only by trying many combinations of Bible readings, rededications, open and closed doors, etc., can they hope to stumble onto it. Some people apparently "hit" the right combination early, but others keep trying, hoping one day to discover the magic formula. They approach God's will almost as if it were a cosmic lottery in which they must purchase tickets until they finally (and accidentally) hit the jackpot.

If there is anything we know from Scripture, it is that God does not play games with us. Whatever pertinent concepts we choose to examine (e.g., calling, guidance, leading, etc.), we find that the biblical record asserts God's eagerness to reveal Himself and His will to His children. Familiar passages (e.g., Prov. 3:5, 6; Ps. 37:4-6, 23, 24; James 1:5, 6) demonstrate God's persistence in granting guidance. Our prayers for guidance, therefore, perhaps ought to be replaced by prayers for insight to recognize the guidance God is already giving.

Persons trapped by this myth enter the decision process disposed to overlook God's daily activity in their lives while they search for the magic combination. If that combination does not appear quickly, they may in desperation resort to the practice of "putting out the fleece." This practice, taken from Gideon's experience in Judges, asks God to grant a sign unrelated to the issue as a confirmation of His guidance. Fleecing is nowhere commanded in Scripture, and even in the case of Gideon was an evidence of weak faith.[2]

We may help persons confused by this myth by (1) teaching about the nature of God, specifically His grace in the daily providence that they overlook as "routine"; (2) showing that the preoccupation with the mysterious is often only an excuse for neglecting self-examination.

Myth: Specific Scripture Verses Give Specific Answers

God has used specific verses in Scripture to call persons into various types of ministry, and their testimonies usually highlight this experience. In addition, believers are frequently told to turn to the Scripture when they need to know God's will about any matter. These factors combine to convince some persons, quite erroneously, that they need a specific verse of Scripture to authenticate any career direction.

While God may use the biblical passages such as those emphasizing evangelism and compassion to call persons into ministry, it is not at all apparent that He means for

---

2. He requested that God twice confirm his commission after God had already given it by special revelation and confirmed it by a miracle (Judges 6:11-22).

the Scripture to be used in that way for all careers. It is doubtful that we can locate specific verses which, taken in context, will direct one into plumbing, accounting, sales, or most other legitimate career options. The teacher who wonders, "Should I teach fourth grade or fifth grade?" will not find the answer in Scripture, no matter how long he looks. Such persons often resort to one of two errors. Either they wrest a verse from its context and distort its meaning in an attempt to gain security, or they assume that the Bible has nothing to say to them and therefore their career path is unimportant to God.

Scripture, of course, excludes several careers from consideration by Christians (e.g., bartender, thief, prostitute, etc.). These specific references give clear guidance *away* from such careers, but there are not equally specific passages that direct us *toward* the vast majority of morally legitimate vocations.

The Scripture's importance in career decision-making is its impact on the decision-maker. Consistent study of Scripture will affect personal growth and self-awareness, make one more sensitive to God, and develop the value systems underlying the decisions. Study of His Word is obviously God's will for all His creatures, and it makes no sense to reject that aspect of His will while asking Him to lead us into His will vocationally. Consistent Bible study will affect the development of such values as the importance of money, security, cooperation, service, competition, authority, recognition, closure, challenge, and probably many more. Such values affect the course of career decisions.

Summary

Myths are held, tenaciously at times, for a purpose. Perhaps the myth, in some cases, is the result of parental or other influence, and the myth holder has simply not been exposed to any other alternatives. In other cases, the myth may be a protective device. The decider may accept the myth of mysticism, for instance, perhaps because of laziness, or perhaps because he fears the results of thorough self-examination. Such motivations must be examined and corrected within the process of dispelling the myths, or the counselee will not be significantly helped.

Myths regarding vocation are dangerous, just as are any other kinds of myths. By their nature they not only deny reality, but also substitute an illusion of reality. Consequently, dispelling such myths is more than a pragmatic matter. Of course, there is pragmatic benefit—better decisions result from understanding reality than from embracing illusion. But we have a prior motivation in that God has called us to know and act upon the truth. Our motivation is not merely "What works best?" but rather, "What is right?" Persistence in accepting vocational myths, therefore, not only impedes the decision process. It also blocks correct and necessary understanding of God, self, and the meaning of work in a God-created world.[3]

3. For a discussion of decision-making and guidance see also Jay Adams, *More than Redemption*, pp. 23-34.—Ed.

19

BOOK REVIEW

Knowing God's Will: Biblical Principles of Guidance, by M. Blaine Smith. Downers Grove, Ill.: InterVarsity Press, 1979. 141 pp. $3.95.

Reviewed by James R. Johnson, Ontario Bible College Library

No simple formulas are given, but this well-written book admirably achieves its purpose of presenting biblical principles of guidance for determining God's will in the complex, nonmoral decisions of life. These are those decisions where moral principles do not settle the issue, such as the choice of which vocation to pursue.

The major thesis is that our usual approach to such decisions should be to use our God-given ability to think logically while fully trusting God to lead us through this means. There is always the danger of falling into rationalism with such an emphasis, but in an age characterized by the opposite extreme of subjectivism such an emphasis is most appropriate. All Christians agree on the need to "trust in the Lord with all thine heart" (Prov. 3:5), but many seem to have understood the rest of the verse to say "and do not use thine own understanding." It actually says "and lean not unto thine own understanding." We are to *use* our minds but at the same time to *lean on* the promise of God's leading. That is the theme throughout this book.

After an introductory section defining the problems involved in making decisions according to the will of God, one section of the book is devoted to expounding the biblical principles of guidance and another section to exposing improper approaches to seeking guidance. Then follows a section devoted to practical, biblically oriented advice on "how we should go about making a logical decision which is glorifying to God" (p. 66).

The basic principles of guidance are presented under the heading "God's responsibility for guidance—and ours." God's part in guidance is simply that—to guide. God promises that He "himself takes the initiative in guiding the person who is open to being directed by him" (p. 29). The Christian must begin with a "tremendous assurance" of this fact.

Our part is "to strive for an attitude of submission to his will," "to spend time in prayer over the decision," "to study the Scripture with respect to the decision," and to "use our God-given reason to make an intelligent choice that seems most glorifying to him" (p. 37). A chapter is devoted to developing each of these themes in its biblical setting. At the heart of the book is the biblical evidence in chapter 7 that "it is through our normal, rational decision processes that we must discover God's leading, provided that we approach our decision making with a willingness to do God's will" (p. 66).

In contrast to these positive principles are two widely misunderstood means of discerning God's will: supernatural guidance through visions, prophecies, and fleeces, and inward guidance by means of intuition or feelings. Several biblical reasons are given why we should not normally expect supernatural guidance, but occasions when such direct leading might be necessary are also discussed. The tendency to look on intuition or feelings as "the sole barometer of God's will" is discounted, however. At the most, such feelings are "merely one factor to be considered along with others" (pp. 81, 82).

The final section of practical advice consists of five chapters devoted to considering personal desires, evaluating abilities, assessing open and closed doors, weighing the counsel of others, and making the final decision. An appendix considers the matter of authority relationships and the will of God. A rigid chain-of-command structure which automatically determines God's will for those under authority is rejected on the basis that the authority of parents, husbands, and spiritual leaders "does not extend beyond a restricted area, and certainly not to our important personal decisions" (p. 127).

Pastors and youth workers will find this book a helpful resource which they will want to share with others. It will prove a valuable addition to the church library. And readers will find it attractive, absorbing, and easily read.

The Ministry of Rebuking

(As It Relates to Church Discipline)

KEITH MEGILLIGAN*

One of the most perplexing problems facing the church today is the inability or unwillingness of its leaders (and nonleaders) to handle internal strife. Far too many cases of sinful behavior/conduct go unattended because the spiritual leadership of a local assembly (or Christian organization) either refuses to deal with the problem or ignores it, hoping (praying!?) that it will go away.

It is probably true, sad to say, that one of the major reasons the problems go unheeded is because of lack of biblical teaching/training in this area. As a result, either the problem is handled poorly, or no biblical solution is achieved. On the other hand, when an attempt is made to resolve the problem, *people* are usually "resolved," rather than the *problem*.

In order to prevent sin from reigning not only in our body (Rom. 6:12), but also in *the* body, sinful behavior/conduct must be dealt with quickly (Eccles. 8:11), firmly (Titus 1:13), and graciously (II Tim. 2:24, 25). The object in handling the matter in this way is not only to evidence biblical conduct and responsibility, but also to restore the sinning brother to fellowship with the body again (Matt. 18:15). There is a need, therefore, to confront the sinner, rebuke the conduct, and, if necessary, discipline the sinning brother.

Rebuke vs. Love

First, it should be pointed out that instruction in godliness is *necessary* if the body is to function biblically. This is true in a positive vein (exhortation) as well as a more negative vein (rebuking). Unfortunately, many Christians in the body of Christ would just as soon ignore this latter observation. But the whole counsel of God must be taught and practiced, and this includes the doctrine of rebuking. If this scriptural balance is not maintained, the body will suffer, "where there is no guidance, the people fall" (Prov. 11:14).[1]

---

* Keith Megilligan is pastor of Grace Bible Church, Berne, Indiana

1. All Scripture references and quotations come from the New American Standard Bible, unless otherwise indicated.

Sadly, problems that develop in the body of Christ are often treated with the "love covers a multitude of sins" syndrome. The closest that one can come to supporting this manner of dealing with a problem biblically is Proverbs 17:9, "He who covers a transgression seeks love.. . . ." and, ". . . but love covers all transgressions" (Prov. 10:12). The problem is, when cited this way these quotations are devoid of the rest of the verse (in each case) and thus lose contextual value. The full texts are:

He who covers a transgression seeks love,
But he who repeats a matter separates intimate friends (Prov. 17:9).

Hatred stirs up strife,
But love covers all transgressions (Prov. 10:12).

In the first passage the writer is trying to maintain the principle of confidentiality between friends. A person who truly loves his friend does not go around telling others about his sinful behavior, but confronts his friend instead. It is not as though he ignores the problem completely. He just refuses to scandalize it to others, preferring to settle it personally.

In the second passage, the point of problem solving is not to lose emotional control (hatred) but evidence loving action.[2] True Christian friends will give of themselves, even risking temporary differences and unpleasantness, to see that the correct biblical action is taken to prevent strife and resolve the problem.

What is that proper action? How does the body of Christ show biblical love toward one who is out of fellowship with the rest of the body because of sinful behavior? By practicing the doctrine of rebuking!

Open Rebuke

Proverbs 27:5, 6 reads, "Better is open rebuke than love that is concealed. Faithful are the wounds of a friend, but deceitful are the kisses of an enemy."

If sinful behavior is to be dealt with biblically, then the most loving thing we can do for our sinning brother is to rebuke him openly, i.e., confront him with the truth. The truth will contain two elements, the nature (description) of his sin and the biblical solution for his sinful conduct. After all, the Bible tells us we treat our friend more like an "enemy" if we do less than this.

Sure, the process is painful (faithful are the *wounds*), no wound is inflicted without some measure of pain; but is our object to *win* our brother (Matt. 18:15) or to be deceitful to our brother? Ephesians 4:15 tells us that when we speak the truth, we should do it "in love." But whatever we do, we must speak the truth! The writer is not trying to dismiss graciousness of spirit and proper timing in handling the matter, but he is trying to emphasize that the matter *must* be handled.

---

2. It should be remembered that the biblical perspective of love is seen in giving (Eph. 5:25; John 3:16; Gal. 2:20) and in action (I John 3:18).

The Nature of Rebuke

What does the Bible mean when it uses the term rebuke? How is it defined?[3] For the purposes of this study, the meaning of the term and its use will be taken principally from the pastoral epistles and in general from the New Testament. The reason for this is the definite application to the conduct and discipline expected in the church of Jesus Christ.

In at least three passages, Paul uses the same Greek word, *elegcho,* which has been variously translated rebuke, reprove, or convict (II Tim. 4:2; Titus 1:13; 2:15). The term means to convict, reprove, to bring to light; also, to disgrace, put to shame, cross-examine, question, accuse, bring to proof. In summation, depending on its context, it would be safe to say that "to rebuke" means to confront with the intent of proving (substantiating) an accusation of unbiblical conduct. And that is what each of these above passages is indicating. The following is the writer's translation:

> Preach the word, be ready whether convenient or not convenient, *reprove,* rebuke,[4] exhort, with all patience and teaching (II Tim. 4:2).

> This testimony is true. For this reason *rebuke* them severely, in order that they should be healthy in the faith (Titus 1:13).

> These things speak, and urge and *convict* (rebuke) with all authority; do not allow any one to disregard you (Titus 2:15).

The message is clear to both young Titus and Timothy, part of your spiritual ministry is to rebuke when it is needed. And, it will be needed! In the case of Titus, Paul had some specific examples (persons) in mind to whom this rebuking ministry was to be applied. It appears from the context, the more severe the sinful behavior, the more severe the rebuking.

Although the II Timothy 4:2 and Titus 2:15 passages list rebuking as a ministry to be applied as needed, it is the Titus 1:13 passage that gives the ministry meaning and purpose. First, the meaning. When it is recognized that the conduct of the Cretans being dealt with here includes lying, acting like beasts, and being lazy, it is small wonder that they needed rebuking. Couple that with the meaning of the term "to rebuke" given above, and it is clearly seen that their conduct needed to be "shamed." Moreover, Paul uses an adverb here to strengthen the application of this ministry—it is the word "severely." Literally this term means "absolutely, precisely, in the strictest sense." In other words, there was to be no question as to the ministry of rebuking or the extent of its application. Since their conduct is confirmed by the testimony of one of their own countrymen, then the rebuking is to be applied "in the strictest sense."

---

3. For a more thorough discussion of this matter, see Jay E. Adams, *More than Redemption* (Phillipsburg, N.J.: Presbyterian and Reformed Publishing Co., 1979), pp. 226ff.

4. Yet another Geek word meaning to censure or speak seriously.

But if rebuking, even as a ministry, served only the purpose of convicting someone of his sinful behavior, it would leave a spiritual vacuum. However, that is not the case. Paul goes on to say (in Titus 1:13) that the purpose for rebuking is to keep the Cretans' faith healthy.

As a biblicist, the writer believes that correct teaching (orthodoxy) yields correct (biblical) conduct. However, when the conduct is no longer biblical, it becomes necessary to correct it. Paul is pointing out in this passage that the ministry of rebuking has a goal or purpose, and that is to get the sinning Christian back on the path of a "healthy faith." To that extent, Paul's use of the term is similar to our Lord's in Matthew 18:15. In that passage the Lord says that a rebuking ministry, applied biblically, should yield the goal of winning our brother.

Every biblical doctrine and ministry ought to have a goal. The ministry of rebuking is no exception. The immediate goal is to win our brother; but if he refuses "to listen" to the ministry or rebuking, then church discipline must take over. In that sense, a higher goal or purpose takes over, that of keeping the church free from "spot or wrinkle, or any such thing" (Eph. 5:27). If the ministry of rebuking does not lead to restoration, then it must lead to discipline. There is no other choice.

Medicine
and
Health

BOB SMITH
Editor

Bob Smith is a practicing physician in Lafayette, Indiana, who also works closely with the Christian Counseling Center in that city.

Is Oral-Genital Sex Sinful?*

Many arguments are given to provide an answer to this question. The difficulty is that most of them are based on emotionalism and preference rather than the correct use of biblical principles. Because specific biblical references are not made to certain problems, many people tend to accuse God of saying nothing on the subject. But He has promised that He has provided all we need for life and godliness through Jesus Christ and His Word (II Pet. 1:3), and that Word provides answers for every aspect of our life (II Tim. 3:16, 17). Even though a specific problem is not mentioned in the Bible, God has given principles and guidelines to use in solving all of life's problems. The subject of oral-genital sex within marriage is no exception. In this article I want to first look at what the Bible says about the subject, and then deal with some problems encountered in it.

Many have stated that the Bible says nothing about oral-genital sex and thus by silence leaves it to man to decide what is right or wrong. In his book, *Solomon on Sex*, Joseph C. Dillow has taken an indepth look at the Song of Solomon.[1] He uses Hebrew commentators as well as other sources of translations in his study. The reader is referred to a review of that book which follows this article for details. Mr. Dillow concludes that in the Song of Solomon God has described oral-genital sex in marriage. Although it is not commanded, it is also not forbidden. The Song of Solomon teaches that it is a normal, natural part of sexual relations in marriage. But there are definite biblical guidelines for its use.

I Corinthians 7:3, 4 teaches that the primary goal of sex is giving to meet the needs and desires of one's spouse. Love focuses upon giving to the one loved. These principles must guide the oral-genital sexual activity. It is not sinful as such, but when these principles are violated, that violation is sinful. The goal of oral-genital sex must be to provide pleasure for one's spouse. To demand it for one's self is selfishness and sin, and to refuse it is also selfishness and sin because each is focusing on self, not the other. Biblical love opens the door to honest communication of desires (without demanding satisfaction of those desires). Therefore, a husband who enjoys oral-genital sex should share the desire with his wife. But, if she has no desire for it, or

---

* This is a very controversial subject. Persons disagreeing with the article should write to the author. Dr. Smith will be happy to entertain responsible, biblical replies.

1. *Solomon on Sex* is the only Christian book I have seen that takes an open, aggressive look at this aspect of sex in marriage. The author is to be commended for the balance he provides.

even dislikes it, he must focus on her desires, not his. The goal of sex for him is to please her, not himself, so to please her he will avoid it and find other ways of satisfying her sexually. His goal cannot be to get from her, but give to satisfy her. By contrast, if she learns that her husband enjoys what she doesn't, she must do two things: first, learn to enjoy it to please her husband;[2] secondly, become more aggressive in other sexual activities. A husband who desires oral sex may be seeking some additional delights in the relationship that arise from his wife's failure to focus on giving to provide pleasure for him. Sex may be routine and allowed (or tolerated) by her and may not provide much satisfaction to him. Oral sex may seem to him to be a way to provide some excitement to a rather routine activity. But he should not need to seek this; a wife following biblical principles of sex should see this as her responsibility and a part of her spiritual ministry to him. Pleasing God means each pleases the other, and this is satisfying to both. Couples with a conflict over oral-genital sex need to change their focus. Regular intercourse is the normal sexual relationship in marriage. Although oral-genital sex is not a substitute for intercourse, it may add to the pleasure or the enjoyment of that relationship (only because of the desire to please one's spouse, not to get pleasure). In most conflicts over this activity the goal of giving has been ignored and both are insisting on their own way.

Some have taken the attitude that oral sex is done only by those seeking to get more pleasure out of the relationship. They conclude that since that goal is wrong, oral sex therefore is wrong. In that context, the action is wrong because of the wrong motive (of course, the action is wrong if done outside of marriage, but this is true of any sexual activity). God doesn't condemn pleasure, because He has given us "richly all things to enjoy" (I Tim. 6:17). But pleasure cannot be the ultimate goal of our actions; that goal is pleasing and glorifying God (I Cor. 10:31; II Cor. 5:9). But if pleasure arises in the process or as a by-product of pleasing God, it is not to be avoided because it is pleasant. We do not take that attitude toward food, clothes, room temperature, etc.; so why should we with sex? In fact, pleasure is an important part of those things, but it must not be the motivating factor. This also applies to sex in marriage in general.

There is a justifiable concern for cleanliness and the transmission of disease by this activity. Good personal hygiene is vital to cleanliness and preventing transmission of disease. Genitalia will need to be cleansed prior to oral-genital activity. This can be a part of the foreplay. The most significant disease to be transmitted this way is the herpes virus. One kind causes cold sores on the mouth and a similar one produces the same kind of sores on the genitalia. The latter has been implicated in cancer of the cervix. Some think that the oral virus can be transmitted to the genitalia. Since this disease may occur through oral-genital sex, some have cited this as evidence for refraining from such activity. This is tantamount to saying that one should not ride in a car because people get killed in cars. The best prevention of disease is avoiding oral-genital sex when such sores are on the mouth or genitalia.

2. See the review of the *Solomon on Sex* for more on this.

Another argument against oral-genital sex is that God did not make people's organs for that purpose. Such a statement is only an emotional assumption. Many organs of the body have multiple functions. The mouth is used for eating, breathing, and talking. There is nothing about it that prohibits it from being used in sexual play. It is a sexual organ when used to kiss, communicate love, or communicate a desire for sex. The penis is used for elimination of urine and as a sexual organ. Since not-infected urine is sterile (free of disease germs), it is actually cleaner than the mouth. The vagina is used as a sexual organ and as a birth passage. It may harbor disease germs, but these rarely find a receptive host in the mouth and intestinal tract of the husband. If a wife has a known vaginal infection, oral contact with her vagina and clitoris should be avoided by her husband until the infection is gone. Even though the rectum is near both penis and vagina, it rarely carries disease germs unless the person is sick. The solution is good hygiene of the genital and rectal area, plus avoiding oral-genital sex when disease is present in the mouth or genitalia.

The world views the concept of "consenting adults" to justify oral sex and other actions. This is not a biblical term, since it implies that each agrees to allow something to be done to him or her. Consenting or allowing is not the goal of biblical sex. Oral-genital sex may be a normal part of the sexual activity in marriage if both agree. This doesn't mean both must agree to do it to each other. One may desire to give and the other desire to receive without the reverse occurring. Oral sex may progress to climax, but it is not to be a regular replacement for intercourse.

Within these guidelines oral sex is not sinful! It can be a pleasant addition to physical intimacy of marriage when following biblical principles. Sin comes from selfishness and demanding personal satisfaction without concern for the wishes of the other.—R.D.S.

BOOK REVIEWS

Solomon on Sex, by Joseph C. Dillow. Nashville, Tenn.: Thomas Nelson. 197 pp., $6.95.

Reviewed by Bob Smith

At last! Here is a book that takes The Song of Solomon at face value and says that this book of the Bible is describing the sexual relationship between the husband and the wife. For years I have wondered why this view has not been taken by commentators on The Song of Solomon. As a young man I had heard my pastor father state that the Song of Solomon could not be read by Jewish children until they were twelve years of age. Even though I have not been able to substantiate his statement, it has still been thought provoking. If it is true, why was this book kept from those children until they came of age? My conclusion was that it describes a very intimate physical relation that was properly not to be a part of the sex education of young children. But it was to be taught (in a proper framework of God's principles) in the early phases of adult life. So, I have looked for authors who would deal with the Song of Solomon from this perspective. *Solomon on Sex* does that in a very superb and practical way for us in the twentieth century and all eras. The author describes the intimacies of the physical relationship and uses *The Song of Solomon* to

help strengthen this aspect of marriage. He states, "The book is full of metaphors and other symbols, but was never intended to be an allegory. Instead, it is simply a picture of idealized married love as God intended it" (p. 9).

Chapter 1 is a description of the origin of the book, its symbolism, and Solomon's qualifications to write it.

Chapter 2 deals with The Song of Solomon 1:1-14. The author of *Solomon on Sex* says this describes the wedding day and the anticipation, by the bride and groom, of the sexual relationship they will enjoy on their wedding night. He uses the practical translation of Franz Delitzsch on many of the words. These words are used to describe the sexual relationship which many authors have seemed to want to avoid. Words like love in 1:2, which refers to sexual love, and embrace in 2:6, referring to fondling and sexually stimulating the body by touch, are found repeatedly in this book. The bride's view of sex is the biblical view of sex; "She obviously was not afraid of sex nor did she have any preconceived notions that sex was dirty, sinful, or hurtful. This sets a keynote of the Song:

sexual love between a man and his wife is proper and beautiful to the Father'' (meaning God). The bride "reflects on how aroused she was and how she had looked forward to making love with her husband on her wedding day. She had a 'holy desire' for her husband'' (pp. 16, 17). The desire is called holy because God created it.

In this first chapter he encourages a person entering marriage to realistically appraise marriage, count the cost of marriage, and make the decision by the will without allowing the emotions to blind decision making (p. 18). Such evaluation prepares for the hard times that do come in the marriage relationship. "Love always involves a sober evaluation of the cost of commitment to a relationship that may not always be easy" (p. 18).

He has an excellent section on modesty and another on dealing with physical problems present from birth. He has practical applications such as his description of the groom's reference to his wife as darling. When Solomon calls his wife by this name, "he links his desire for her with his protective love and care. Protection and love go hand in hand. A woman needs to feel protected, because protection gives her security, and the more secure she is, the freer she is to love unreservedly. Very often the woman who feels secure in her husband's love and protective concern takes great delight in sex with her husband" (pp. 22, 23).

Chapter 3 is a description of their activity in the bridal chamber on their wedding night. Again, Dillow uses the Hebrew words to describe the relationship.

This is the first book that I have read in which the author communicates a proper appraisal of 2:3. This author is not hesitant to suggest that "here we have a faint and delicate reference to an oral genital caress" (p. 31). Regrettably, his words are not as strong as they might be. On page 9 he has suggested that the way to understand this book is to take it at face value, and this needs to be done with this particular verse. It is not a "faint" reference but a strong reference to oral-genital sex, since this is a description of the sexual relationship. He says that the word "fruit" may refer to male genitals or semen. The bride states that as she anticipates for this she "takes great delight" in it, because she will be providing pleasure for her husband. Since pleasing him was delightful to her, she found his fruit (referring either to his genitalia or his semen) was sweet to her taste. This means that it was pleasant to her because the activity provided pleasure for her husband. This needs to be carried one step further. She found the oral contact with his organ and the semen actually sweet and pleasant to her taste buds. Women who are repulsed by this may have a wrong view of the sexual relationship. Some of them may be forced into this relationship at the husband's insistence, which causes them to view it as unpleasant duty of satisfying their husbands' physical desires without any love being involved. But a wife who sees it as pleasing her husband can develop a taste for his genitalia as has been described by this passage in The Song of Solomon.

In chapter 3 the author strongly emphasizes the need for premarital chastity in 2:7. He also has a very practical section on bedroom atmosphere, which is something many people tend to ignore. Yet it was a very important part of the sexual relationship between Solomon and his bride.

He also very aggressively approaches the subject of limits in marriage. He sets three rules. First of all, unselfish love must be the motive. Secondly, there must be mutual agreement, and thirdly, there must be mutual submission. In these three things he is saying that the goal of any activity must be to please the other without demanding satisfaction for one's self.

In chapter 4, which he entitles "Time of Preparation," he covers 2:8 to 3:5. This is a reflection of "certain events leading to her marriage with Solomon as well as some problems they experienced in the early years of their marriage" (p. 42). In this chapter the author presents two reasons, which he gleans out of The Song of Solomon, for abstaining from premarital sexual involvement. The first reason is that "to do so may jeopardize the beauty of sex in marriage" (p. 43). The second reason is that "it tends to obscure one's objectivity in making the correct choice of a life partner" (p. 43). Then the author gives three basic purposes from The Song of Solomon for the engagement period. "First, it is a time of getting to know one another in ways other than sexual (2:8-14). Secondly, it is a time of coming to grips with the potential problem areas of a couple's relationship and establishing problem-solving procedures (2:15-17). Third, it is to be a time of seriously counting the cost

of being married to this person (3:1-5). Too frequently young people today get married on a wave of sexual passion, with no clear picture of the person they are committing their lives to" (p. 43). "If you cannot work out problems you do know about before you are married, it is almost certain you will not be able to resolve problems you do not know about until after you are married" (p. 47). "A dating relationship can be structured around inexpensive and creative fun (such as picnics by a river) that provide opportunities for each partner to really get to know one another and to talk out in detail their feelings about life, their commitment to Christ, and their basic views and backgrounds. The purpose of the engagement period should be related to getting to know your future mate well" (p. 49).

"Sexual passion has a way of sweeping a person into marriage or an emotional tie without getting to know each other first of all in ways other than sexual. The obsession of sexual desire tends to tempt a girl and guy to spend more time petting than working out the 'little foxes' and problems that need to be worked through before the marriage commitment is made. Also, the power of aroused sexual passion can drive a couple to get married without giving serious thought to the problems of life with that person after you have said 'I do' " (p. 51).

The author lists seven excellent questions to be considered when one is looking over a member of the opposite sex for his qualifications for marriage. These questions involve commitment to Christ, a right view of priorities, right views of authority, finances, and sex, as well as the ability to respond properly when one is hurt or offended by someone else. This is a very useful chapter on premarital counseling, with two major exceptions. One is that he seems to allow the arousal of sexual passion before marriage if a couple is committed to go through with the wedding. This seems to be an obvious contradiction of all the things he has said about the difficulties arising from such a relationship. It also fails to take into consideration that marriage is the only license for sex. A commitment to marriage is not permission for sex. The second weakness in this chapter is his dependence upon temperament differences as a source of problems. This concept ignores the real cause of these problems and makes it easy for one to excuse behavior on the basis of a temperament which is believed unchangeable. In addition, it does not provide a solution for these problems.

In chapter 5 the author describes the significance of the wedding ceremony. Chapter 6, described as "The Wedding Night," covers The Song of Solomon 4:1–5:1. In this chapter he describes the intimacies of the sexual relationship that occur within the confines of marriage. In The Song of Solomon there is a complete lack of inhibition between the husband and wife. The wife in this book of the Bible did not believe that being "sexy" or erotic in her relationship with her husband was wrong. In fact, she took advantage of such a relationship to increase the pleasure of the sexual activity. There was the knowledge that God had de-signed the sexual relationship with intense pleasure as part of it. In The Song of Solomon both people knew that this pleasure was the by-product of their relationship. They did not do as many do today and focus primarily on technique in order to get or increase pleasure. Such an emphasis has caused others to become anti-technique in their relationship. Many people think that since the world focuses on technique to increase pleasure, believers should not be concerned about it. Since God designed the relationship to be pleasant and designed the husband and wife with capabilities to produce pleasure in it, neither should be hesitant to do those things which increase the pleasure of the spouse. Throughout The Song of Solomon that is a very vital part of the husband-wife relationship. Dillow takes advantage of its suggesting various ways husband and wife can increase pleasure for each other.

In this chapter the oral-genital relationship is again discussed. Dillow uses the Hebrew scholar Franz Delitzsch as his resource in his interpretation of the Hebrew language. I have attempted to find out if these translations and interpretations by both Delitzsch and Dillow are accurate and have been unable to find anyone to tell me that they are incorrect. I want to comment on these statements and then attempt to place the whole concept in balance. The author has set the stage for oral sexual relationship in the early chapters of the book. In pages 80-87 again are found the references that may speak of the oral-genital relationship. The author has stated that the garden refers to the wife's vagina

(p. 82). In Song of Solomon 4:16, the wife describes a fragrance that comes from her garden, signifying that the vaginal secretion has a pleasant odor which will be appreciated by her husband's face near that area. The same verse suggests that her beloved eat fruit in her garden, which again is a description of the oral-genital relationship. Fruit may describe the pleasure of the sexual relationship, but it also may (since fruit is to be eaten) describe the contact of the mouth and the vagina. Since the entire book is a picture of the sexual relationship, it seems very difficult to exclude this part of the picture. On page 84 the author, in describing the significance of the "streams from Lebanon" (Song of Solomon 4:15), refers to Proverbs 5:16, where that phrase is found and there signifies male semen. In Proverbs 5:15 drinking is a part of the relationship which may refer to participation in sexual activity and may also continue the picture of the oral-genital relationship. Since The Song of Solomon refers to the oral-genital relationship producing semen (which is ejaculation), and that same concept is found in Proverbs, it appears that the Scripture is describing the wife having oral sexual contact with the husband to the point of his ejaculation. Some wives do not enjoy the taste of the husband's pre-ejaculatory discharge nor of the ejaculation products themselves. But this is like many things in life that a person learns to like when he desires to. Many foods are not liked when they are first eaten, but after a period of repeatedly ingesting them a desire and an appetite for them are developed. When a wife realizes that this relationship is pleasing to her husband, she will learn to like it, not because she wants to for her own benefit, but because she wants to do that which is pleasing for her husband. She can develop a taste for this that is comparable to her desires for foods that she has learned to like.

Much attention has been drawn to the oral sexual relationship in marriage. Regrettably, unbelievers have been the ones to cause Christians to focus on this area. As is true in many of the sexual relationships, abuses by nonbelievers of certain aspects of sex do not mean that this is wrong within the marriage relationship. God has given us, in His Word, all the instructions we need to provide a vibrant sexual relationship in marriage. Because nonbelievers focus upon physical life as the sum total of life, they attempt to put as much pleasantness in that life as possible. Many Christian marriages are not taking advantage of all the principles of God's Word, with the result that there is not much pleasantness in their relationship. When they see the wrong focus of the world, they erroneously conclude that pleasure is not to be a part of sex. They also erroneously conclude that because the world does various things in its attempt to increase pleasure in a sexual relationship, those things are automatically wrong within marriage. This is doing what many believers do in allowing the world instead of God's Word to dictate standards.

It has been alleged that this view of The Song of Solomon is twisting it around to justify a position. Proponents of this argument insist that the book must be considered an allegory or metaphor of some kind. It is unclear why they insist that it can be only one kind of allegory and not allow other types of allegories. If it is an allegory of the relationship of Christ and the believer, the husband-wife relationship is also an allegory of the relationship of Christ and the believer. God has developed the sexual relationship as an expression of love between husband and wife. I have often wondered if the pleasurable delights of the sexual relationship are also a picture of the pleasurable delights between Christ and the believer. I believe that an emotional dislike of the oral-genital relationship has colored honesty in the use of the Scripture. I am also afraid that such an emotional view of the relationship is behind most of the arguments that are propounded against it. That emotionalism also interferes with the placing of the oral-genital actions in a proper relationship within marriage.

Even though The Song of Solomon refers to the oral-genital relationship, it is not a command to do so. The Song of Solomon is describing what happens with a husband and wife who are deeply committed to the goal of providing intense sexual pleasure for each other. It is also describing the balance that must be in a marriage sexual relationship. The goal of the sexual relationship is not getting, nor is it achieving climax, nor is it pleasure. The goal of the sexual relationship, according to I Corinthians 7:3, 4 is giving to meet the needs and desires of one's spouse. For a husband to demand oral sexual relationship against his wife's wishes is violating biblical principles and is thus a sin. The Scripture no-

where condones damanding anything in the sexual relationship. Such a view is selfish and as selfishness is therefore sin, even though the sexual activity is not condemned by the Scriptures. My statements are directed to husbands because it seems that most of the problems in this area stem from male insistence upon this act. But for a wife to refuse to be involved in this relationship when she knows it is something pleasant to her husband is equally sinful. Her goal should not be to avoid what she does not like, but to give to please her husband. The standard of sexual conduct is not to be demanding what one wants, but desire to meet the desires of the spouse. A list of personal desires should be drawn up by each person of the marriage relationship and then given to the spouse. When that list is turned over to the spouse, the right to have even one item on the list is also given up. If a husband lists receiving oral-genital pleasure from his wife as something he desires and she fails to provide this for him, she is violating the principle of God's Word to please him. Thus she is sinning against God in failing to use her body to please her husband according to I Corinthians 7:4. For him to demand that she do it is also sinful, because he is seeking his own desires and is not concerned with her desires. When he gives her the list with such a request on it, he gives up all right to it, and if he never experiences it, that is between her and God. He cannot demand it (although he may discuss it with her), since his goal is not to be receiving pleasure. His goal is to be giving her pleasure according to her desires. When his wife receives the

37

list with this on it, her goal must be to provide her husband with pleasure in this way, even though she might not derive pleasure from this action. Wives do many things that are not necessarily pleasant, and some are even unpleasant. But there is joy and satisfaction in being responsible and doing them because they are contributing to the life of someone they love. Many wives refuse to apply this reasoning to the oral-genital relationship. For one to refuse to do so because she does not like it, because it does not taste good, or for any other reason is wrong. He has not demanded it; he has listed it as something he enjoys, and her goal is to give to please him. She may need to learn to like it to be the kind of wife that pleases God. This doesn't make it the dominant factor of the sexual relationship, but one of those nice acts that take advantage of the pleasure that God has designed. Since the husband hasn't demanded it, the wife is free to be creative in this area and use her body to please her husband. By not demanding it, he is leaving the responsibility on her shoulders before God. He is to love her without regard for what she does for him. His goal is also to please his spouse, so he is to satisfy her sexual desires in the ways she has on her list. If she does not want oral sexual relationship, he must leave this area completely alone.

This raises a problem to many people. If he says he desires oral-genital sex from his wife and she doesn't, how do they settle it? The goal is giving, and this is the guideline to use to reach a solution. He has stated his desire but is not demanding it. He is merely stating a fact.

Knowing his love is not dependent on whether or not she satisfies the desire, she is free to avoid it if she desires. But as a loving wife she is not to function from her desires, but his. Yet, she knows he will not demand it for two reasons. She has stated her desire to avoid it, for one, and secondly, love forbids demanding for selfish goals. So he makes no further issue of the topic to honor her request and satisfy her desires, but she will seek to satisfy his desires and provide oral-genital sex for him.

The principles listed here are the principles that are to guide all sexual activity in marriage. The goal is giving to please the spouse, not getting one's own pleasure. Pleasure is the by-product of giving, not the goal. Believers need to learn the biblical principles for sex that are clearly set forth in I Corinthians 7:3, 4 and make them the dominating factors of their life. "In order for sex to be an expression of love, the needs and desires of the other person should be more important than your own" (p. 79). Open, honest communication is essential in this.

Chapter 7 is a strong emphasis upon these concepts. Here Mr. Dillow adds I Corinthians 7:3-5 to what The Song of Solomon is saying. "It is sin to reject your mate's sexual interests (actively or passively)." "When we eventually got to the root of it [rejecting a mate's sexual interest], there was generally a problem of selfishness and sin somewhere" (p. 106).

Another important aspect growing out of this Scripture is also mentioned by the author on the same page. "It is interest-

38

ing that throughout The Song of Solomon and in I Corinthians 7 there seems to be an underlying assumption that there is no real difference in the sexual needs or drives between men and women. As far as the Bible speaks to the issue, a woman's need is viewed as equal to the man's." "The capacity and desire for sex is equal" (p. 106).

"One reason so many men appear to be obsessed with sex is because they get so little of it from their wives. If a man hasn't eaten in five days, every time he passes the refrigerator food is all he can think about. Like food, sex isn't the most important thing in life; but if you are not totally available, it can become an obsession to your husband." "The central issue in sexual love is not having an orgasm; rather it is sharing mutual love" (p. 107).

The author continues this further in chapter 8, entitled "Solving Sexual Problems": "The solution to their differences involved assuming personal responsibility for the error rather than focusing on the other's error" (p. 111). "When you and I stand before the judgment seat of Christ, He is not going to ask how our mate treated us, but whether or not we were faithful in assuming responsibility for our behavior. It is God's responsibility to deal with an offending mate, not ours" (p. 112).

"Whatever tensions may have developed in their relationship (5:4-6), they do not appear to affect Solomon's expressions of love and praise for her. Most husbands, when rebuffed after making a sexual overture to their wives, tend to withdraw into a shell or react in a 'cut-ting' way. But Solomon demonstrates true love, always responds properly, and lovingly demonstrates much patience and confidence in the Lord to work things out" (p. 119). Song of Solomon 6 shows how he did this. "To adopt this kind of attitude shows Solomon truly loves her as Christ loves the church (Eph. 5:25). Christ loves us consistently regardless of how we perform. That does not mean the Shulamite should not improve her performance if it needs improving, just as we need to improve our performance in our relationship to Christ." "Part of having a sexual relationship with your mate in an understanding way is not to respond with insult when hurt, but to respond with blessing —with love and appreciation for his or her strong qualities" (p. 120).

As The Song of Solomon shifts to the satisfaction Solomon has with his wife (6:8, 9), from I Corinthians 7:5 Dillow focuses upon the responsibility of the wife to provide that satisfaction. "The best prevention for adultery is complete satisfaction at home." A godly wife in a message to a group of women said, "A prostitute is skilled in all the techniques of giving sexual pleasure to a man she does not even know or love. If they can do that for a man they do not know or love, just for money, surely we should be even more skilled in giving sexual pleasure to our husbands whom we do love" (p. 122). Wives are encouraged to have a right attitude about the sexual relationship with their husbands. The author encourages them to have the right kind of thought life to aid this activity. "It is perfectly 'holy' to think erotic, sexual thoughts about your husband during the day. It's in the Bible. Too frequently women who cannot climax tend to view their husband's genitals as separate from their husband as a person. They would never daydream about their husband's body as Shulamite did; it seems repulsive to them. This is a major cause of orgasmic dysfunction. You are to consider his genitals as part of him as a person. You are to consider his semen as life, his life! This is easy to grasp in connection with conception and pregnancy, but not in regard to sex" (p. 129).

One short statement on page 128 summarizes the source of most sexual difficulties. "Sexual problems are usually relationship problems." This is saying that sexual difficulties occur because of a failure of the husband or wife to be the kind of person they should be and do not think of the other the way God desires.

Chapter 9 is a description of the wife in an uninhibited display of her body to her husband. In this chapter he shows how the biblical relationship in sex is completely uninhibited. Since it was the wife in this chapter who is acting in a very aggressive, uninhibited manner, Mr. Dillow spends a considerable amount of time talking to wives about this aspect of their lives. The uninhibited behavior of the wife in The Song of Solomon was goal oriented. "She was being creatively aggressive to please her man" (p. 140). Some claim that this is not their nature or their personality. This is a cop-out for being responsible sexually. It is necessary for her to change to please her spouse. "God would have an inhibited wife change her personality a little and

strive to be what her husband needs!" (p. 140).

"Paul taught that sexual intercourse was to picture Christ and the church (Eph. 5:31-32). This is an astounding parallel and certainly ought to have forestalled the common notion that Christianity is against sex. What is the essence of the parallel? Death! Paul said the husband was to love his wife as Christ loved the church and gave Himself for her. The believer is told that in denying himself and losing his life, he will paradoxically find it (Mark 8:35). Mutual death to self is the key to total oneness spiritually and physically.

"To what does the wife need to die in the physical realm? She needs to die to inhibition. Inhibition is sometimes a subtle form of rebellion. Paul says the wife no longer has authority over her own body and the husband no longer has authority over his. Once you are married, your mate owns your body (I Cor. 7:4). Thus, inhibition is insisting on an authority that you no longer have and thus is sin.

"The husband, on the other hand, needs to die to the feelings of embarrassment or awkwardness in expressing tenderness and romance. Both must die for the intimacy of the total oneness of sexual love to be experienced. You both die to anything that would obstruct your mate's pleasure" (p. 143).

The author then states there are "three basic keys to fully satisfying your man sexually." These are (1) be more aggressive; (2) be totally available; (3) be creative. "It is biblical for a wife to be a skillful lover to her husband." "The young man of Proverbs 5:19 is told to be drunk with his wife's sexual skill!'' This skill 'involves taking the initiative' '' (p. 146). To give further insight to this he refers to his wife's book, *Creative Counterpart*.

The concluding chapter of the book deals with the concluding verses of The Song of Solomon. The author here describes some general aspects of love.

The book concludes with two appendixes, the second of which is an interpretive outline of The Song of Solomon based on the author's view of it. In an addition there is a one-page chart breaking down the details of this outline into a summary form.

Appendix I deals with solving problems involving sexual dysfunction. This is a fairly good section with the weak points coming from the author attempting to mix Freudian psychological views with biblical solutions to problems. For those who desire to use this section in counseling I will comment in detail about the strong points and the areas to avoid in counseling. He has three basic parts in this section: (1) Four General Attitudes to Avoid; (2) Premature Ejaculation; (3) Orgasmic Dysfunction.

The four attitudes to be avoided are (1) blaming your mate; (2) the spectator's role; (3) goal-oriented performance; (4) myths. His statements under blaming one's mate are excellent. ''The problem is not yours, or hers, or his; it's your relationship that needs treatment.'' ''Obviously, the inter-personal interactions of all sexual problems play an enormous part in the cause and solution to sexual problems.'' ''So, stop thinking *he*

has a problem or *she* has a problem; it should be *we* have a problem'' (p. 159). ''You see, your mate's problems are your problems because you are one, just like Christ and the church. The proper attitude is, 'Let's both of us go to a counselor and see if we can get some insight into our problem' '' (p. 160).

As a spectator one may become concerned about his response and thus focus upon himself. The author states, ''Instead of getting totally involved physically with one's mate, forgetting everything else and just 'letting' sexual arousal happen naturally, a person may mentally set himself apart and observe his own responses.'' This occurs because an individual may be afraid of failure in response. The author is too weak in dealing with this problem. The solution is to quit focusing on one's own response, or one's own pleasure received in the relationship, and to focus on giving pleasure to the spouse.

Similar statements are made when the author discusses goal-oriented performance. Here also, failure of response is being evaluated. The goal-oriented performance is important as long as the goal is pleasing the spouse. Dillow does not focus upon this as strongly as he should.

The fourth attitude to be avoided is accepting myths about sexual relationships. He states, ''the only way to avoid them is to become sexually informed'' (p. 161). This is very true, as there are many, many erroneous myths about sexual activity which must be set aside to develop a good relationship.

The second subject he deals with is premature ejaculation. The steps to the solutions are fairly accurate and have been proposed by Masters and Johnston, and are also described in detail by Dr. Ed Wheat in his book, *Intended for Pleasure*. He does give some rather idealistic goals that are not necessary and are actually impossible for most men to achieve. He states, "a husband should be able to enjoy fifteen minutes of continuous thrusting and be able to build to thirty minutes of actual intravaginal containment (not continuous thrusting). This doesn't necessarily have to characterize every lovemaking session, but you should have this capacity if you and your wife are going to experience all the sensations God intended a husband and wife to enjoy in their love" (p. 162). For him to say that a husband "should be able" or "should have this capacity" is incorrect. This is something that a husband may seek, but if he does not obtain it, he is not an inadequate husband, nor is he missing "all the sensations God intended for the husband and wife to enjoy in their love."

The last section of the Appendix (which occupies three-fourths of the Appendix) deals with orgasmic dysfunction. He gives twelve steps to correct the problem. In general these steps are very good. The strongest ones are: (1) become factually involved; (2) as a couple, commit "your" problem to the Lord; (3) re-establish communication; (8) overcome inhibitions; (9) exercise and develop the P.C. muscle; (10) develop tactile sensation without any intention of moving to orgasm; and (11) practice structured genital sensation.

Probably the weakest one is step 4, in which he tries to deal with the origin of orgasmic dysfunction as being a negative feeling toward men. Here the Freudian concepts are prominent and are erroneously presented as the cause. This also appears in step 6, where he attempts to present a biblical view of men and the male role. He regrettably accepts the conclusion of a female psychiatrist as to the cause of orgasmic dysfunction in women. Admittedly there may, in the past, be some very great environmental stresses in a woman's life to which she has responded erroneously, but the difficulty is an unbiblical response and an unbiblical view of sex in the marriage relationship. Her view of sex and her husband especially needs to be confessed as sin, and she needs to take the biblical view in this area. To accomplish this the author attempts to get the wife to surrender her role as a separate step, but the solution is more than surrender. The solution is becoming aggressively involved in solving the problem. The reason a woman is not having climax is because of her wrong view of the sexual relationship. Very likely she and her husband seek climax as the goal. Many husbands think they have not completely satisfied their wife unless she has an orgasm. This is an unbiblical view of the sexual relationship. Simply stated, the solution to this problem (which has been erroneously labeled frigidity) is focusing upon the biblical view of marriage and sex. The goal is not for the wife to have good feelings, or orgasm, but to give to meet the needs of her husband. Because of the closeness and the intimacy of the relationship, many wives find that inter-

42

course without climax is very satisfying. A wife needs to focus on the giving relationship and allow her body to relax as she focuses upon the satisfaction and joy of pleasing God in giving to meet the needs of her husband. As she turns her focus from what she is experiencing to what she can give, the tension she has about various aspects of the sexual relationship will be removed. In time she will find the giving to be very pleasant, and from this it is only natural for climax to occur. As the author has stated, there needs to be open communication between husband and wife. This means she shares her desires with her husband. If she has no desire for orgasm, he must be willing to stop. It also means that she focuses upon giving to please him and learns to be as uninhibited as necessary. If a wife were to look at the things she does for her husband as pleasing God and therefore pleasing to her, she would find more satisfaction in these things. She needs to develop the attitude that what excites her husband is exciting to her.

The fact that she is exciting him by doing certain things should excite her. The author focuses upon some helpful procedures such as developing the P.C. muscle and having her husband stimulate her in a relaxed and non-demanding way. His last step in the solution is intercourse with the female in the above position, which gives her more control. This may or may not be that necessary. He does have a right goal when he concludes the Appendix in the section with this statement, "It will be necessary for the wife to satisfy her husband during each session, but her orgasm is not to be the objective until it just happens as the culmination of all the steps" (p. 182).

In general this is an excellent book. It sits at the top of the list along with Ed Wheat's book, *Intended for Pleasure*, as one to be used in dealing with sexual problems in marriage. There are probably very few marriages that couldn't be helped by both husband and wife reading this book and applying many of the principles that are given here.

The Act of Marriage, by Tim and Beverly LaHaye. Grand Rapids, Mich.: Zondervan Publishing House. $3.95.

Reviewed by Bob Smith

This book of 294 pages is an attempt to describe "The Beauty of Sexual Love." It is also an attempt to present a biblical view of the sexual relationship in marriage. As is true of many of these books, the authors mix contemporary psychological views of man with the biblical view of man. The result is very confus-ing for one who does not know where to turn for answers. Psychological views are more frequently opinions than they are facts. This book takes many of these contemporary opinions and philosophies of man and adds Scripture to them, but does not give a solid biblical view of the sexual relationship. There are 13 chapters (which will be briefly covered in this report), with a 14th chapter devoted entirely to questions and answers. A three-page bibliography is the conclusion of the book.

Chapter 1, entitled "The Sanctity of Sex," has many good points. The statement found in Genesis 1:28, "be fruitful, and multiply, and replenish the earth," "was given before sin entered the world; therefore, lovemaking and procreation was ordained and enjoyed while man continued in the original state of innocence." "It is reasonable to conclude that Adam and Eve made love before sin entered the garden."

"God created all parts of the human body. He did not create some parts good and some bad; He created them all good, for when He had finished His creation, He looked at it and said, 'It is all very good' (Gen. 1:31)" (pp. 11, 12). "God is the creator of sex. He set human drives in motion, not to torture men and women, but to bring them enjoyment and fulfillment" (p. 14). "Some people have the strange idea that anything spiritually acceptable to God cannot be enjoyable." There is "no reason why a couple cannot pray before or after a spirited time of loving" (p. 15, 16).

The author presents four central principles that are taught in I Corinthians 7:2-5:
"1. Both husband and wife have sexual needs and drives that need to be fulfilled in marriage.

2. When one marries, he forfeits control of the body to his partner.

3. Both partners are forbidden to re-fuse the meetings of the mate's sexual needs.

4. The act of marriage is approved by God" (p., 19).

Two glaring problems are present in this chapter and one continues throughout the book. The one is the title of the book and what that title says. The authors have entitled the book, *The Act of Marriage*. In doing so they are defining the sexual relationship as the essence of marriage. Other terms are used such as "lovemaking," "make love," and "loving." All such terms are used in this book to refer to the sexual relationship which says that love and sex are synonymous and interchangeable. This is certainly far from the truth. Sex is not all there is to love, and love is not expressed only through sex. The act of marriage is not the sexual relationship. The act of marriage is the binding of two people together in a lifelong companionship, and as a result of that bond the sexual relationship will be a very vital part of their life. But the act of marriage is not limited to or centralized in the sexual relationship.

This is also seen in the other problem, which is the authors' view that "The wedding ceremony in itself is not the act that really unites a couple in holy matrimony in the eyes of God; it merely grants them the public license to retreat privately to some romantic spot and experience the 'one flesh' relationship that truly unites them as husband and wife" (p. 12). Many people have taken the erroneous and unbiblical view that marriage is not complete until the sexual act has been accomplished. It is regrettable

44

to see how the Roman Catholics have been allowed to influence our philosophies about sex. In the Scripture marriage is not dependent upon the sexual relationship. However, the sexual relationship is dependent upon marriage. Marriage in the Scripture is commitment to meet the needs of one another. As a result of that commitment the sexual relationship will occur, but the marriage is completed at the completion of the legal ceremony. It does not need a sexual relationship to make it a bond. The Catholics have used this view to provide various unbiblical ways of dealing with conflicts that occur in marriage. Marriage is far more than a sexual relationship. The Scriptures repeatedly teach of the spiritual unity that occurs between the husband and wife, of which the physical relationship is but an illustration.

In chapter 2, entitled "What Lovemaking Means to a Man," and chapter 3, "What Lovemaking Means to a Woman," the authors attempt to emphasize the significance of sex in a marriage relationship. However, they get it all out of priority and make it the *basis* for a good relationship instead of the *result* of a good relationship. In the chapter for the husband they essentially end up saying that good sex produces a mental well-being, fulfilled manhood, good love, good relationship, and good excitement in his marriage relationship. As one reads the chapter it appears that sex is the key to man's success in life. This is easily seen in the following statements. "A sexually satisfied husband is a man who will rapidly develop self-confidence in other areas of his life" (p. 23). "A

sexually satisfied husband is a motivated man" (p. 30). Although sex is important in marriage, this view does not give hope or guidelines for those who are not having their desires satisfied by their mate. If one does not have that kind of sex that has been described in chapter 2, it appears that there is no need to continue living. There is inadequate attention given to companionship in marriage, which is basic to a successful sexual relationship. The result of the LaHayes' focus is that people will seek to make sex the secret of their success instead of the biblical principle that it is the by-product of marriage success. They are really saying that a good sex life is what makes a good marriage. What they communicate is that marriage oneness is accomplished through sex. This is not biblical and is actually the world's view of the sexual relationship instead of God's view.

In chapter 3 the same philosophy comes through. Sex is presented as the ultimate expression of love, as the glue that holds marriage together. It is very regrettable to see such a philosophy presented. This is what the world has been saying. When this excitement is not retained in marriage, people conclude the glue is gone and they are free then to fracture the marriage. This philosophy communicates that one's experience is far more significant than what the Word of God teaches about marriage and sex. In addition, the concept of self-acceptance shows up through the book and becomes another of the goals of a good sexual relationship. Saying that good sex produces good self-acceptance in essence is saying that the goal of sex is getting. Self-acceptance, self-worth, and self-esteem have been discussed previously.[1]

The authors attempt to accept what psychology has to say about the human make-up and then make it fit biblical concepts. This is found on page 37, where they say "the one point on which psychologists agree is that all people have the basic need to be loved." Regrettably, they do not say that God loved us first and His love is all that we need in order to function. They imply that we must be loved by other people in order to function properly.

Throughout the book are found many sayings of men which are accepted as correct philosophies for dealing with people. "A sage once said, 'A woman is the most complex creature on the earth.' Certainly no reasonable man would claim to understand her fully" (p. 34). This is in contradiction to I Peter 3:7, which says that a husband must live with his wife according to knowledge. He must know his wife, he must learn about her, and she can be understood. Some might argue that the authors are emphasizing the word fully; however, in reading on the emphasis is seen to be on understanding. These kinds of philosophies are found sprinkled throughout the book and become the basis of what the authors say in many areas.

Chapter 4, entitled "Sex Education," is a fair chapter on the anatomy and physiology of the sexual organs. Regrettably, the descriptions are not very accurate and

1. See the previous issue of *The Journal of Pastoral Practice* for a review of this concept as presented by Dobson.

the diagrams are inadequate for those who have little or no understanding of the human body. In this chapter the authors encourage an indepth study of the sexual relationship by a young couple prior to their marriage. In fact, those statements are found under the paragraph heading, "Learning by Doing." After stating that they should study this prior to marriage, they state, "God didn't give Adam and Eve a manual on sexual behavior; they learned by doing" (p. 45). A couple who is committed to meet each other's needs does not need an indepth study of the sexual relationship before marriage. They can discuss attitudes, and they need to discuss various results of the sexual relationship (i.e., children), but an indepth study of the sexual relationship itself is unnecessary prior to marriage. What is best for them is to take one or two good books about the sexual relationship on their honeymoon and spend that time in reading, learning, and experimenting with their own sexual desires, needs, and functions. Any desires stirred up by their reading of books can be satisfied, since they are married at that time. It is placing undue stress upon them to focus upon the sexual relationship in such detail prior to marriage. In fact, it is unfair to them, because it is saying that if they do not have a good sex life they cannot have a good marriage.

Chapter 5 has a title which is regrettable for reasons stated previously. It is entitled, "The Art of Lovemaking." The authors are not talking about love, but are discussing the sexual relationship, which is one of the expressions of love. Lovemaking is not limited to the sexual relationship. In this chapter the authors attempt to describe some of the physical changes that go on in the sexual relationship. The LaHayes make some excellent points in this chapter. Here they do get down to the fact that a couple should study books about the sexual relationship during their honeymoon. They correctly encourage the couple to plan the honeymoon where they can be away by themselves with adequate time to learn about the sexual relationship. Interestingly, they encourage an afternoon wedding, which gives them leisure time alone (after the ceremony, prior to bedtime) in which to relax and prepare for the first sexual encounter that may happen that night. But they present enough erroneous material in this chapter to make it more detrimental than helpful. For one thing, they teach that the ultimate objective in the sexual relationship is orgasm for both husband and wife. They increase this error by adding that simultaneous orgasm is the "ultimate in lovemaking" (p. 72). This is a goal that is not biblical or proven to be physically necessary. Many women have great satisfaction from the sexual relationship without achieving an orgasm in every intercourse. There are many couples for whom it is quite difficult to have simultaneous orgasms and who find that one preceding the other does not in any way reduce the satisfaction from the relationship.

A give-to-get philosophy grows out of the section on foreplay, in which they point out that foreplay arouses one's wife and as a result the husband "will attain in her response intense excitement himself,

and it will enrich his own climax" (p. 65). There is nothing wrong with the husband seeking this as long as this is not his primary goal. If the goal of his foreplay is to increase his wife's enjoyment and pleasure, and his own pleasure comes as a by-product of this, the statement by the LaHayes is then correct. But it's easy for this personal gain to be the reason for the foreplay, and as such it becomes a wrong goal.

Chapter 6, entitled "For Men Only," and chapter 7, "For Women Only," have lists of good aids to the sexual relationship. However, the goal for these is wrong. "The following suggestions will guide husbands in helping to create in their brides a wholesome appetite for lovemaking" (p. 82). There is nothing wrong with these things if they please her. But the author presents them here as ultimately being for the husband's benefit. I don't mean to be picky, but many times people subtly communicate unbiblical philosophies in their statements, as this does. However, the items listed are very good for a husband to use in meeting his wife's needs and desires. They are as follows:

1. Learn as much as you can.
2. Practice self-control.
3. Concentrate on your wife's satisfaction.
4. Remember what arouses a woman.[2]
5. Protect her privacy.
6. Beware of offensive odors.
7. Don't rush lovemaking.
8. Communicate freely.

2. This should be more specifically what arouses your wife.

9. Love your wife as a person.

This is an excellent list and fulfills biblical criteria in a husband being the kind of husband he should be in a sexual relationship.

The list for wives is almost equally good.

1. Maintain a positive attitude.
2. Relax! Relax! Relax!
3. Chuck your inhibitions.
4. Remember that men are stimulated by sight.[3]
5. Never nag, criticize, or ridicule.
6. Remember that you are a responder.[4]
7. Observe daily feminine hygiene.
8. Communicate freely.
9. When all else fails, pray.[5]

It is interesting that the women are to pray when all else fails, but not the men. The difficulty with this chapter is that they again communicate the philosophy that the only happy and contented men are those who are satisfied sexually. They communicate that the basic source of happiness in marriage is sex. They do not talk about these things being done to please God, but for a wife to please her husband and, in so doing, to remove the pressure from his wrong views of sex. This is a give-to-get philosophy.

Chapter 8, "The Unfulfilled Woman," deals with what has been mislabeled as the "frigid wife." A fairly good list of the factors hindering a wife's achieving orgasm is given. The chapter

3. This is a learned behavior, not the way they were created.
4. A wife is also to be aggressive in the relationship, as taught by I Corinthians 7.
5. And, according to Philippians 4:6-9, start thinking right and acting right sexually.

fits the pattern for the rest of the book, with some accurate statements and many inaccurate ones. Regrettably, the authors do not give a clear solution to the problem presented. In addition, the wife's goal appears to be getting the climax rather than pleasing her husband.

In chapter 9, entitled "The Key to Feminine Response," the authors give a fairly good description of the muscles of the outlet to the vagina and its effect upon the sexual relationship, but it is not the key that unlocks the door to all pleasure.

In attempting to deal with the sexual problems the husband encounters, the authors, in chapter 10, "The Impotent Man," are very authoritarian without any authority behind it. On page 122 they attack modern psychology for avoiding God in dealing with man's problems. "A subject that modern psychology overlooks today in its humanistic efforts to solve man's problems independent of God is the reality of conscience." But throughout the chapter they repeatedly referred to so-called "truths" which are really conclusions reached by psychologists and psychiatrists. A few of these follow. "Researchers in this field almost invariable report that fear of castration is a universal problem with men" (p. 159). "A man is regularly plagued with five great sexual fears." "A man cannot accept being unattractive to his wife" (p. 160). "A man simply cannot accept ridicule." "One can be certain that if a man is small when soft, he fears being inadequate" (p. 161). They also encourage self-forgiveness, which is not a biblical concept (p. 163). In an attempt to justify all these, they state on page 180, "Remember that all truth is God's truth. Regardless of its source, truth is truth. Einstein's theory of relativity should not be negated because the author was a humanist. In the same manner a liberal medical treatise read with spiritual discernment may furnish prompt solution." They don't realize that the so-called "truths" learned from psychology come from man's attempt to evaluate man (created in the image of God) without God. This is markedly different from Einstein's view. Einstein was not looking at the behavior of man, but was looking at the creation. The philosophy that the LaHayes have is that it is all right to look at man without God, determine his behavior as a creature apart from God, and then use those conclusions along with biblical philosophies. All truth is truth *if* it is *truth*—as measured by the standard of God's Word. Just because a statement is made by a certain scientific group does not make that statement truth. Because a so-called authority makes a statement that (to many people) is acceptable as truth, this does not make it truth.

Chapter 11, "Sane Family Planning," has some fairly good information, but is not complete in that it ignores some other concepts, including sexual interstimulation.

Chapter 12 presents the results of a survey that the LaHayes made of people with whom they have contact. This information is interesting but doesn't necessarily mean these are the normal responses in sex. Chapter 13 is the gospel presentation under the title, "The Missing Dimension." Chapter 14 is the long chapter, "Practical Answers to Common Questions." This follows the pattern of the book, with a mixture of strong and weak points present throughout. One of the major weaknesses is a failure to give biblical principles in answering problems. Where they find no specific comment about a problem, they state that the Bible is silent on the subject, but then do not give biblical principles to use in answering questions. This is regrettable, coming from a pastor. In this section they again encourage self-forgiveness, which is not a biblical concept.

Although they believe the Bible does not have any guidelines in dealing with masturbation, they do come out with a good list of reasons why it is not an acceptable practice for Christians. Their view of abortion makes it possible to encourage the use of the IUD as a form of birth control.

In general this book is a mixture of good and bad. Unless a person is skilled in identifying unbiblical philosophies, it would be easy to accept what is stated here as coming from the Scripture and thus teach it as a right view of the sexual relationship. There are some things a pastor may use in this book for resources, but he has to be careful (when it comes to philosophies and descriptions of anatomy and physiology) to make certain that these are as accurate as the author claims they are. As a physician, I cannot recommend this book as a book to be read by couples who are having sexual difficulties. I prefer using other books, which have been referred to elsewhere, for that purpose.

100 Ways to Defeat Depression, by Frank B. Minnirth, States Skipper, Paul D. Meier. Grand Rapids, Mich.: Baker Book House, 1979. $1.95.

Reviewed by Bob Smith

It is depressing to read a book on how to handle depression that does not really solve the problem. This paperback of 100 pages (many of which are not even half filled) by its title suggests depression may be defeated in 100 different ways. As I read books of this kind, I find it difficult to avoid being extremely negative, first, because of the mixture of anthropologies, and second, because they do not deliver what they promise. The Word of God teaches that the way to deal with problems is to put off the old unbiblical behavior by replacing it with biblical behavior that is pleasing to God. The authors of the book (apparently believers) no doubt have a sincere desire to help other Christians deal with problems. One cannot fault them for their desire and their compassion for people. However, their background in psychiatry and their unwillingness to recognize the influence that psychiatric anthropology has had on their use of God's Word reduce this book to pious platitudes. Each page has a Scripture verse which has much to do with dealing with depression. But the authors either water it down or extract so little from it that they fail to give any real guidelines on how to use it to defeat depression. The sum and substance of the book seems to be that if one trusts in God, meditates on Him and His Word, the depression will somehow magically leave.

The book does correctly deal with some changes that must be made, but very few of the put-off/put-on principles are found. The authors do attempt to *comfort* the depressed person through Scripture, but little hope is provided other than somehow through God's magically producing improvement in their lives. Throughout the book one is repeatedly *told* that God will help (and God's ways are past finding out—Rom. 11:33), but this is without any responsibility on the part of the individual. Where requirements are given, the reader is not told how to accomplish those responsibilities.

Some of the strongest statements on the part of the authors are on page 13, where they describe behavior as the cause of one's feelings. They also strongly take issue with the word "can't" on pages 22 and 58, and show that the Scripture says we can do what God requires of us. In dealing with behavioral changes that must be a part of dealing with depression, they very strongly talk about changing the focus from one's self to others and their needs on pages 65, 66, and 67. In dealing with anger, they use the verses of James 1:19, 20 and teach that we must be quick to hear and slow to speak. On page 93 they correctly use Matthew 6:34 in helping people deal with worry by focusing on today's problems. This is essentially the sum of the good concepts present in this book.

The greatest fault in the book is the typical attempt of many (if not most)

Christian psychiatrists and psychologists to mix psychiatry and psychology with the Bible. When one realizes the unbiblical anthropology of these philosophies, it is clear that it is impossible to mix these two ways of approaching problems. Statements alleging that God desires the removal of certain psychiatric conditions are repeatedly found *without proof* from the Scripture. These may be seen on pages 25, 38, 58, 79, and 80. Psychiatric jargon is present throughout the book. These include such terms as inferiority feelings (25), work-a-holic (27), suppressed inferiority feelings (27), ventilation (45, 72), lowering of self-esteem (55), self-love (60), negative programming (68), self-forgiveness (77), self-esteem (79), false guilt (80), unconscious motive (81), negative self-concept (89), and subconscious (97). If such terms are needed in helping people deal with problems, it follows that Christ and Paul did not do a very good job, since these terms were not available to them.

The book deals with 100 items, some of which take two pages. Since there is no other page numbering, the total number of pages is unknown. These 100 are broken into seven different topics. In each of these topics, each item is separately titled. Part One has 25 items entitled "Developing a Better Relationship with God." The first seven are entitled "Draw Close to God." This is stated as something needed, but the how-to is missing. Numbers 8 to 23 are entitled "Trust God," and 24 and 25 are entitled "Depend on God."

Numbers 26 and 28 are "Focusing on Christ," which is the total of Part Two.

Part Three is entitled "Focusing on God's Word." The titles found in this part are "Meditate on God's Word," "Live by the Counsel of God's Word," "Recognize the Supernatural Power of God's Word," "Hold Fast to God's Promises," "Fill Inner Emptiness with the Joys of God's Word." All of these sound very profitable, but not much practical help is found. The main thrust is to read, memorize, meditate on God's Word, but there is very little on application. Again, it seems that spending time in God's Word is a magic wand that will remove depression. References to application, doing, and change (which the authors limit to thinking) are found only once each in 32, 35, and 38 respectively.

Part Four, from 44 to 49, is entitled "Praying for Help and Guidance." Subtitles here are "Be Bold to Call on God," "Express Your Problems to God," "Be Assured God Will Answer You."

Part Five, from 50 to 55, is entitled "Avoiding Satan and Sin." Subtitles here are "Be Aware of the Techniques of Satan," "Resist the Devil," "Avoid Sin."

Part Six, from 56 to 67, is entitled "Drawing Strength from Others." The subtitles are "Learn from Others Who Have Been Depressed," "Draw Close to Your Mate," "Develop Friendships," and "Help Others." Regrettably, the authors make getting from others the goal of the development of the friendships, which is in direct contrast to the biblical goal of helping others.

Part Seven, "Dealing with Faulty Individual Life Patterns," extends from 68 to 100. Many of the subtitles list things that contribute to depression and should be handled, but there is not much biblical instruction on how to deal with them. The subtitles themselves seem to offer more solutions to the problems than the authors' comments.

It disturbs me to write this kind of report, but I don't know how else to handle books like this. Believers who are unwilling to admit that the anthropology in which they've been trained is unbiblical cannot possibly offer significant help that has eternal benefits in the lives of others. I do not desire always to be negative, but I am concerned about the attempts to mix unbiblical philosophy with biblical teaching. This gives an air of credibility to the unbiblical philosophies and turns people away from the Word of God, which tells us repeatedly that God has provided all we need for life and godliness (II Pet. 1:3).

Medical News of Interest
To the Nouthetic Counselor

LIFE EXPECTANCY CLIMBS
TO NEW RECORD

Americans' average life expectancy at birth reached "an all-time high of 73.3 years in 1978, and the age-adjusted death rate and infant mortality reached record lows."

"Since 1950, about three years have been added to the life expectancy of older individuals. A person who was 50 years old in 1978 may expect to live to age 78, and a 65-year-old person to age 81." Death rates were higher for men than women, but the gap is narrowing. White women are expected to outlive white men by 7.7 years.

"The rank of the 15 leading causes of death did not change between 1977 and 1978." The three leading causes of death are heart disease, which caused 38 percent of all deaths, malignant neoplasm, which caused 21 percent of deaths, and blood vessel disease.

"When all causes of death are included, Alaskans have the lowest and Floridians the highest mortality in the United States. The average Alaskan is much younger and the average Floridian is much older than the average American." The median age of all Americans was calculated as "28.1 years in 1975; the median age in Alaska was 22.9 years, compared with 32.3 years in Florida."

"Nevada, with its casinos and easy divorce laws, has the country's highest suicide rate in the United States (24.8/100,000 residents). But statisticians are keeping an eye on New Jersey's rate (7.2/100,000 residents), which was the lowest before gambling was legalized there. The national average is 12.5 suicides per 100,000 population."[1]

---

1. *Family Practice News* 10, 23:2, 35.

"EFFORTS TO STAMP OUT SMOKING APPEAR TO BE DRAGGING"

"Although significant advances have been made in the diagnosis and treatment of lung cancer, progress has been slower in attacking the major causative factor, cigarette smoking."

"Cigarette smoking is the primary cause of 80% of all bronchogenic carcinomas in men," and the impact of smoking can be influenced "by brand, presence of a filter, tar content, duration of smoking, and depth of inhalation."

"Anti-smoking campaigns have succeeded in getting an estimated 30 million Americans to quit smoking, and teenage smoking, which has increased in the 1960's, showed a decline of 25% between 1974 and 1979."

"Cigarette advertising budgets remained astronomical, and approximately 54 million Americans still smoke, indicating that efforts toward prevention and cessation of smoking must be increased. More than 100,000 will die from lung cancer this year, and using current rates, the projected estimate for the year 2,000 is 300,000 deaths annually. The rate of increase of lung cancer has declined slightly in men, but is still increasing in women."

In this article it was stressed "that the mortality from lung cancer remains tremendous," and "the fact that the irrefutable link between lung cancer and cigarette smoking continues to be rejected, at least in practice, by a large segment of society" was strongly decried.

Society has "successfully crusaded for reduction in industrial and community pollution, but we have not directed sufficient effort against the greatest health hazard of all."[2]

ADOLESCENCE & PREGNANCY

"One in 10 adolescent girls become pregnant each year." "Nine of 10 adolescents who become pregnant before the age of 15 drop out of school." "Pregnant teenagers who drop out of school before they turn 15 have an excellent chance of having a second child by the time they're 17."

"Many pregnant adolescents starve themselves so that they can still wear blue jeans, participate in school activities, and not look different from their peers."

"Adolescent mothers often become isolated and depressed and look years older than their age. Different from their peers and different from young mothers in their twenties, they feel they don't fit in anywhere."[3]

---

2. *Family Practice News* 11, 2:61.
3. *Family Practice News* 11, 2:90.

HEALTH IN THE YEARS AHEAD

"For the coming decade, Americans can expect healthier futures with longer life expectancies; they will see reductions in both infant mortality and deaths due to heart disease and strokes," according to the Department of Health and Human Services' 1980 annual report on health trends in the United States.

But the health picture is not trouble-free. Certain types of cancer are on the increase, particularly respiratory, breast, colon, pancreatic, and bladder cancers, and there is a rise in deaths due to accidents, especially by motor vehicles, "which accounted for 50% of accident deaths."

Heart and blood vessel disease "remains the leading cause of death in the United States," but mortality, based on age-adjusted death rates, declined 20% in 1970–1978. This was due to declining heart disease mortalities in the younger age groups; a 30% decline for each group in the 25-44 year range and a 20% decline for each succeeding age group.

"Cancer, the second leading cause of death, showed an increased overall mortality of 6% from 1950 to 1978."

"Accidents, the fourth leading killer, led the top of the list as the main cause of death for those under the age of 35. Seventy-five percent of the deaths in this age group were caused primarily be motor vehicle accidents, by other accidents, homicides, and suicides."

Medical costs in dealing with these diseases "could be further cut through more preventative action such as reducing cigarette consumption, controlling high blood pressure, and recognizing poor nutrition and the misuse of alcohol. If preventative actions were successful in cutting direct and indirect cost expenditures by only 10% reductions would still equal billions of dollars."[4]

---

4. *Family Practice News* 11, 4:5.

Missions

MILTON FISHER
Editor

Milton Fisher is professor of Old Testament and president of the Reformed
Episcopal Seminary, Philadelphia. He was formerly a missionary to Ethiopia.

A Modest Proposal
For a Grand Scheme

Psalm 67 expresses a plea based on the confident expectation that God will surely prosper His people among and above all nations.

> God be merciful unto us, and bless us;
>   and cause his face to shine upon us;
> That thy way may be known upon earth,
>   thy saving health among all nations.
> Let the people praise thee, O God;
>   let all the people praise thee.
> O let the nations be glad and sing for joy:
>   for thou shalt judge the people righteously,
>   and govern the nations upon earth.
> Let the people praise thee, O God;
>   let all the people praise thee.
> Then shall the earth yield her increase;
>   and God, even our own God, shall bless us.
> God shall bless us; and all the ends of the earth
>   shall fear him.

Expression of so great an assurance, extensive in scope and expansive in magnitude, even to most Christians sounds like hyperbole. We prefer to "spiritualize" or idealize such verses—or to relegate them to a future eschatological dispensation. Or perhaps, rather, we can take it as past history, God dealing with His earthly people Israel in a manner not to be expected in the New Testament age. But wait. Is not this the very sort of psalm we ought to view as prophetic, as partaking of a universality which demands we seek its realization in the spread of the gospel of Christ?

If, however, the universal proclamation of the way of salvation and the acknowledgment of Israel's God in joyful worship finds its fulfillment in our age, then how about the consequent visible blessing of God—the earth yielding her increase? Indeed, it follows *in the psalm itself* (last verse) that, in consequence of His blessing, "all the ends of the earth shall fear Him." That's a missions success story if there ever was! There is to be so tangible and undeniable a reward from God to the faithful that others will be turned to Him in faith and reverence, out of conviction that His Word is true. He produces what He promises.

But how does this demonstration of God-given prosperity, the earth yielding her increase, come about? Will Christians, in particular, be led to discover rich oil deposits or diamond mines or veins of gold? If so, the spirit abroad these days could lead more to an increased resentment than to a submission to God. Will Christian farmers have more abundant rain, for the increase of their crops? Hardly! That would be in conflict with the Scripture, which tells us He sends his rain on the just and on the unjust *alike*.

The special missionary project, if we might call it that, which I am championing in this article is that a modest start be made at what seems the best if not *necessary* approach to witness in Third World nations today. If Christian technicians, engineers, and business men would make available their skills and expertise, so much in demand in backward and developing regions, several things could result at once. First, they themselves would gain entrance and constitute a presence free of the stigma which the "missionary" often bears. Second, they could give tangible evidence of the honesty, dependability, and hopefully the superiority of a Christian performance and product. This would in due time be followed up necessarily and effectively by vocal testimony to the spiritual motivation behind such performance. Third, and far from least significant, the establishment of a business or industry in a land with only a few local believers could provide training, employment, and a new respectability for an otherwise depressed and despised Christian minority. Their own lives would thus be blessed with prosperity, and their witness would become far more viable.

Where might this begin? Progressive nations like Chinese Taiwan, Thailand, Indonesia, perhaps even Japan, would be ready to accept some specialized foreign investment, including operational personnel. Even better prospects would be areas such as North Africa, Persian Gulf states, India, and Pakistan. Central and South America could use such a helping hand, though here as elsewhere caution is called for with respect to involvement in unjustifiable political sponsorship, political instability, and arousing of resistance to "Western imperialism" (now called "neoimperialism"). Yet the *Christian* entrepreneur should be of such caliber as to overcome the "ugly American" self-interested stereotype. The sense of uncertainty and insecurity bred by political instability ought not be considered a real deterrent. Risk has always been part of the missionary venture. In particular, the Christian commercial firm or contractor must be wise enough not to align itself inextricably with government factions.

The modern pastor needs to keep abreast of current trends in world evangelism. He has to be ready to counsel young Christians faced with hard choices as to how they may best satisfy the demands of Christ's commission, "Go into *all* the world," in such a day as this. Where and how does one go forth into a world with "Go home, Yankee" fever? The proposal made in this article is one possible answer. WILL IT WORK? Has it been tried? Is anyone doing anything of this sort? Yes, yes, and yes to these three questions.

Your missions editor does not want to make this sound like his own private and original idea. He is only being careful to protect the anonymity of the source(s) of his information—for obvious reason. What follows, even more than what has been suggested so far, is based upon confidential information about just such Christian business operation now in existence in more than one of these hard to penetrate regions. Let's call it "the Father's business."

That there is a valid reason for Christian enterprise in "hostile" environments is fully realized by those already committing their energies to it. Hitherto, Christians of "sending countries" have been affluent enough to finance not only their own missionaries (though this has now become increasingly financially burdensome in many locations) but also to subsidize the local churches planted by them as well. The situation in much of the Third World now, however, is such as to disfavor or forbid continuation of this method of missionary endeavor. The very term "missionary" is increasingly a bar to entry or a stigma and distraction from genuine witness. It can be harmful to the independent growth and support of the indigenous church; not that this ought to be the case, but it sometimes is.

In the Muslim world, for instance, the doors to conventional missionary work are closed or closing. It is imperative that an alternative means of Christian witness be found. Pastors in our American churches should be made aware that such an alternative does exist and is already demonstrating its effectiveness. If one were to translate Paul's "tent-making" into the modern context, a reasonable analogy would be "business," the organization of capital and skills to provide goods and services as a normal means of livelihood in a community or country.

Three assumptions underlie the application of this scriptural analogy to the operation of modern missions. (1) Business endeavor (commerce, industry, etc.) provides the income (salary or profit) for the vast majority of urbanized persons and, hence, indirectly provides income for churches and their missions outreach by way of Christian stewardship. (While a few Christian minorities in Islamic communities, such as business minded Ismailis and Parsis, are able to support their own churches, believers are an economically depressed group in most situations, and therefore much in need of employment and training opportunities.) (2) While "making money" cannot be an end in itself for any committed Christian, business is a truly legitimate activity for Christians, as long as it is carried out within the legal bounds set by secular authority and the moral bounds set by the law of God. (3) Happily, the business world is a "neutral" arena in which Christians naturally mix with others and can build the kind of relationships in which mutual respect can be shown for those of different convictions. In particular, the life of each person comes under close scrutiny for several hours every day. For the Christian, then, this affords an excellent opportunity to share his faith, by manner of life and even verbally, as occasion arises. For the Christian employer and managerial level personnel this includes various business associates and contacts, some of whom may never have had real association with Christians before.

Now contrast the above principles of Christian endeavor with standard Christian missions, thought of mainly in terms of either full-time church work (evangelism, Bible teaching, etc.) or recognized Christian social service (education, medicine, etc.). None would question that such activities are essential and valuable in themselves. They are a central part, though not the entirety, of the total mission of the church as Christ's body in the world. The church itself will remain impoverished both materially and spiritually, however, if Christians attempt to work along these lines alone. This is certainly true in the majority of communities of the Muslim world, where traditional avenues are largely closed, alternative ones becoming not only desirable but *essential* to a continuing Christian witness.

One company already in operation has established the following goals and policies:

(1) To provide the opportunity for both foreign and national Christian professionals to work in certain countries, finding occasions for active witness in everyday life within the business world. This witness touches a group of people not normally reached by the churches.

(2) To uphold Christian ethical standards in a generally corrupt business environment, and to produce work of the highest quality.

(3) To establish *locally*, not as a foreign firm, that the business be fully indigenous, not subject to the vagaries of changing policies toward foreign-based companies.

(4) To provide work for both local Christians and nationals of other persuasions to create daily contact for the dispelling of misconceptions and opening of channels for communication of the gospel. A particular objective is the provision of on-the-job training in various skills for the raising of working and living standards.

(5) Since the aim of a Christ-centered company is not the financial enrichment of its owners, profits are channeled into further Christian work through a legally established charity trust.

(6) The essential product of this and similar companies will serve to visibly improve the quality of life for the entire community thus served.

NOW THAT YOU'VE READ THAT, do you see why Psalm 67 was selected as a fitting "text" for this presentation? Do you still wonder how in the world (especially the Third World) American churches and her individual Christians can ever fit the picture?

Let me suggest three possible ways of involvement for any Christian whose imagination is captivated by this perfectly natural and practical plan with such dramatic potential for Christ's kingdom. First, he could apply as an individual to become part of an existing enterprise—or influence another to make such a move. Second, he could rather plan to start a commercial project of his own, guided by the experience of those who have already engaged in a similar undertaking. Or, third, he can invest some capital in a company already in operation overseas. That request has been set before both British and American Christian groups just recently. He can thus receive a modest percentile of return, recognizing that he can literally invest in foreign missions without giving up anything but the differential between this investment and some other which might afford a greater rate of return.

The name of the engineering company we have in mind cannot be divulged here, for reasons indicated above, but if more information concerning investment or participation is desired, readers can contact me through the Journal, and I can provide a channel of communication. Kindly use official church stationery to identify your Christian affiliation when you write to me and in any subsequent contacts.—M.C.F.

Para
Christianity

WESLEY WALTERS
Editor

Wesley Walters is pastor of a congregation in Illinois. For over twenty-five years he has devoted much time to the study of the cults

Trinitarianism—
A Pagan Creation?

An Examination of Dr. Victor Paul Wierwille's Claim

JOHN P. JUEDES

Dr. Victor Paul Wierwille, in his book, *Jesus Christ is not God,* takes a radically unorthodox stance regarding the Trinity. In his view, Jesus is not God, and the Trinity never was a valid Christian teaching. Is he correct?

The purpose of this study is to critique just chapter 1 of Wierwille's book, entitled "The Origin of the Three-in-One God." This chapter claims that primitive Christian church history never mentions the Trinity. Its origin was not divine revelation, but pagan influence. The study below presents a summary of Wierwille's argumentation, evaluates his quotations and sources, and addresses his main arguments. The primary source is "The Origin of the Three-in-One God." The sources Wierwille quotes will be emphasized in this critique, examining them more broadly and thoroughly than Wierwille does. In addition, some prominent historical works will be brought to bear on the issues at hand.

Summary of Wierwille's Argument

In chapter 1 of *Jesus Christ is not God,* entitled "The Origin of the Three-in-One God," Paul Wierwille attempts to use Christian church history to demonstrate that the idea of the Trinity was a pagan doctrine that was developed and promoted by church leaders until the church formally adopted it as Christian doctrine. Trinitarian heresy caught on and became the cornerstone of the Christian faith only by many ungodly turns of events. Wierwille's discourse on the heretical origin of the three-in-one God entails four basic arguments. He first asserts that "the idea of a triune god or a god-in-three persons was a common belief in ancient religions."[1] He cites the Romans, Babylonians, the Greek triad of Zeus, Athena, and Apollo, and especially the Hindu "trinity" of Brahma, Vishnu, and Shiva. Wierwille maintains not only that non-Christian religions, but also ancient cultures accepted a triune god. Without

---

1. Victor Paul Wierwille, *Jesus Christ is Not God* (New Knoxville, Ohio: American Christian, 1975), p. 11.

specific supporting evidence, he claims that the cultures of the Babylonians, Egyptians, Phoenicians, Greeks, Indians, Chinese, Japanese, Icelandans, Siberians, "and others" are themselves evidence of "how deeply rooted in human thinking this notion was."[2]

Secondly, Wierwille alleges that "the trinity was not a part of Christian dogma and formal documents of the first three centuries after Christ."[3] He further asserts that not even individual church leaders spoke of the Son as equal with the Father, without beginning and unchangeable.

Wierwille's third argument takes the next logical step, transferring trinitarianism from paganism to the church. Since, he says, the pagans accepted a trinity, but the early church did not, pagan converts must have gradually incorporated pagan trinitarian ideology into church teaching. The previous beliefs of the pagans quickly corrupted pure Christian doctrine and practice. As evidence for the recession of true Christianity, Wierwille cites biblical examples of men who fell away from the faith. Individuals such as Hermogenes and Demas, as well as major sects such as the Ebionites and Gnostics infiltrated the church with "idolatrous worship and theories."[4] With this infiltration came loathable insertions of the trinitarian formula into the writings of the church. Even great early works such as the Gospel of Matthew, the first letter of John, and the Didache contained no references to the Trinity until centuries after they were written. Wierwille declares that later persecutions forced the Christian apologists such as Aristides and Justin Martyr to make heretical compromises to paganism in their dissertations, especially the compromising acceptance of trinitarian belief.

The final establishment of trinitarian doctrine, Wierwille says, came through Emperor Constantine, who exchanged political favors for "a strong voice in Church affairs."[5] His pressure alone at the Council of Nicea forced the bishops to accept the trinitarian doctrine promoted by the pagan minority in the church. Wierwille sums up his four basic arguments regarding the heretical rise of trinitarian belief:

> Clearly, historians of Church dogma and systematic theologians agree that the idea of a Christian trinity was not a part of the first century Church. The twelve apostles never ascribed to it or received revelation about it. So how then did a trinitarian doctrine come about? It gradually evolved and gained momentum in the late first, second and third centuries as pagans, who had converted to Christianity, brought to Christianity some of their pagan beliefs and practices. Trinitarianism then was confirmed at Nicaea in 325 by Church bishops out of political expediency.[6]

---

2. Ibid., p. 12.
3. Ibid.
4. Ibid., p. 16.
5. Ibid., p. 22.
6. Ibid., pp. 25, 26.

Documentation for Pagan Origin of Trinitarianism

Where does Wierwille find support for his radical condemnation of trinitarian doctrine and massive reinterpretation of church history? His work is not heavily documented; this chapter averages only slightly over one footnote per page. Many of his notes refer to common-knowledge information, simple history which does not directly support his unique interpretations. Most disturbing, however, are the quotations, which he lifts out of their contexts in order to use them in a way far different than the original author used them. A brief look at his notes follows.

The majority of his footnotes refer to simple history. Note 6 only quotes Acts 21:20, although this verse does not refer directly to Ebionites, as he would have it. Note 7 refers to Hase[7] as a description of Gnosticism (although it is strange that Wierwille cites 18 pages while Gnosticism is covered in only a portion of them). Note 9 reflects the corruption of I John 5:7, 8 which is found in the King James Version, which *The Companion Bible*[8] describes, and which is commonly known and corrected in contemporary translations. Footnote 10 simply refers the reader to a larger discussion of baptism found in another of Wierwille's books.[9] Note 11 refers to Walker's discussion of the edict of Milan and its advantages for Christians.[10] Note 12 cites Hase again, this time to support the statement that Arius was deposed by a synod at Alexandria in A.D. 321.[11] Footnote 13 refers to Chadwick's popular history of the church, which states the Eusebii's connections to Arius.[12] Notes 14 and 15 cite Chadwick again on Os[s]ius' mission to Alexandria and his stance with Alexander against Arius.[13] Note 18 mentions the A.D. 381 council at Constantinople, and note 19 gives the text of "The Nicene Creed" (which he neglects to label more accurately as the Nicaeno-Constantinopolitan Creed).

In five of Wierwille's 19 footnotes, he misinterprets the content or the intent of the authors he quotes. The first footnote in the chapter, "The Origin of the Three-in-One God," is a good example of missing the intent of the writer. Wierwille asserts that ancient pagan religions believed in triune gods, citing Alexander Hislop for proof.[14] This reference and the context of this chapter and book lead the reader to think that

---

7. Charles Hase, *A History of the Christian Church* (New York: D. Appleton and Co., 1886), pp. 53-71.

8. *The Companion Bible* (London: The Lamp Press Ltd.), p. 1876.

9. See V. P. Wierwille, "Baptism," *The Bible Tells Me So* (New Knoxville, Ohio: American Christian Press, 1971).

10. Williston Walker, *A History of the Christian Church*, rev. ed. (New York: Charles Scribner's Sons, 1959), p. 101.

11. Hase, *A History of the Christian Church*, p. 111.

12. Henry Chadwick, *The Early Church* (Grand Rapids: Wm. B. Eerdmans Publishing Co., 1968). p. 129.

13. Ibid., p. 130.

14. Alexander Hislop, *The Two Babylons* (New York: Loizeaux Brothers, 1959), p. 16.

Hislop held trinitarianism to be strictly pagan, and in no way scriptural, Judaic or Christian. However, the very paragraph in Hislop which Wierwille uses against trinitarian doctrine asserts a firm belief in the Trinity. What Hislop refutes is not the Trinity, but the vain attempts of the Roman Catholic Church to use a triangle to represent the King eternal. Hislop's following paragraph minces no words, as it calls the Trinity "the same great truth" and condemns only *representations* of it:

> . . . all such representations of the Trinity necessarily and utterly debase the conceptions of those, among whom such images prevail, in regard to that sublime mystery of our faith.[15]

Hislop agrees that pagan forms of the Trinity show that it is deeply rooted in human thinking. However, he attributes this to the fact that God revealed Himself as Trinity from the beginning. Paganism did not "create" the Trinity:

> While overlaid with idolatry, the recognition of a Trinity was universal in all the ancient nations of the world, proving how deep-rooted in the human race was the primeval doctrine on this subject, which comes out so distinctly in Genesis.[16]

He further states that the Trinity was "the original patriarchal faith."[17] To Hislop, God's people did not adopt pagan doctrine; instead pagan religion continued to teach divine revelation from the beginning, but shamefully perverted it:

> The ancient Babylonians held, the modern Hindoos still hold, clear and distinct traditions of the Trinity, the Incarnation, the Atonement. Yet, who will venture to say that such nominal recognition of the cardinal articles of Divine revelation could relieve the character of either the one system or the other from the brand of the most deadly and God-dishonoring heathenism?[18]

Perhaps Wierwille's most devastating quotation is drawn from the *New Catholic Encyclopedia*.[19] The reader is almost stunned to see the Roman Catholics admit that, according to Wierwille, "trinitarianism became part of Christian doctrine in the fourth, not the first, century."[20] It appears that even Catholics agree that the "Trinity" was "created" three hundred years after Christ! Wierwille apparently does not understand the point that the Catholic article was making, nor does he understand the differentiation between the words "doctrine," "dogma" and "theology." Wierwille's misinterpretation of this source will be discussed in detail below.

Wierwille also appears to misrepresent Hase in one section. He infers that Hase holds that the Christian faith was quickly corrupted by pagan converts.[21] But Hase

---

15. Alexander Hislop, *The Two Babylons* (London: A.&C. Black, Ltd., 1932), p. 17.

16. Ibid., p. 18.

17. Ibid.

18. Ibid., p. 282.

19. *New Catholic Encyclopedia*, 1967, s.v. "Trinity."

20. Wierwille, *Jesus Christ is Not God*, p. 13.

21. Footnote five: Charles Hase, *A History of the Christian Church* (New York: D. Appleton and Co., 1886), pp. 53-71.

does not assert this, and especially does not dub the Trinity a pagan doctrine.

Without any evidence, Wierwille writes off the *Didache*, a well-known early Christian doctrine, as an "example of modified doctrine" with "foreign elements."[22] Wierwille then quotes chapter 7 of the *Didache*, footnoting the section to Harry Rimmer.[23] The reader is left with a very low view of the *Didache*, as well as the implication that Rimmer also sees the *Didache* as corrupt and unreliable. However, just the opposite is the case. Rimmer actually asserts the great reliability of the *Didache*:

> Among all the sources of sub-apostolic literature, this work is the most valuable . . . the most important single document in this field. . . .[24]

Rimmer, who seems to be much better acquainted with the *Didache* than Wierwille, does not see its chapter 7 as "foreign" to the Christian faith and "modified." Rather, Rimmer states of the trinitarian formula and baptismal instructions:

> We have here an authentic insight into the teachings and practices of the Apostles of our Lord concerning the Christian sacrament of baptism. This historical value of such information cannot be over-estimated.[25]

Wierwille once again mistakes the words of an author in his citation of Bettenson in footnote 16 of "The Origin of the Three-in-One God."[26] Wierwille cites this author to support his theory that the Nicene Creed was "truly the work of a minority," and then directly quotes Bettenson in the footnote:

> Arius and his followers were forthwith banished to Illyria and his works were burned. The reverberations of this treatment of Arius had a profound effect on the Church, as well as on Constantine, for several decades. Just as Arius was to have been pardoned by Constantine and reinstated in the Church, he died.

Although this data is basically true, these words cannot be found in Bettenson.

Although Wierwille's footnotes appear to show formidable support for his peculiar church history, close examination reveals many difficulties. Most of the accurate quotations reflect common knowledge data. Others reflect Wierwille's misunderstanding or misuse of the authors' content or intent. In fact, of the dozen authors Wierwille cites in his treatise against the historical veracity of trinitarian doctrine, only one is as anti-trinitarian as he is.[27] None of the other historians, many recog-

---

22. Wierwille, *Jesus Christ is Not God,* p. 17.

23. Harry Rimmer, *Crying Stones* (Grand Rapids: Wm. B. Eerdmans Publishing Co., 1946), p. 99.

24. Ibid., pp. 80, 77.

25. Ibid., p. 99.

26. Henry Bettenson, ed., *Documents of the Christian Church,* 2nd ed. (London: Oxford University Press, 1963), p. 58.

27. The anti-trinitarian is Alvan Lamson.

nized in their field, interpret or present the data as Wierwille does in "The Origin of the Three-in-One God."

Primary Arguments Discussed

Some of Wierwille's key arguments need to be examined. First there will be a discussion of his tenet that paganism had trinities which predated and influenced the Christian church. The second discussion revolves around whether early church leaders viewed Jesus Christ as inferior to God. The third discussion focuses on the key issue of "doctrinal development" in the Christian church. This is the crux of the whole issue, as Wierwille takes a different view of doctrinal development than the church had and continues to hold.

Trinitarianism: A Pagan Creation?

One of Wierwille's underlying assumptions is that if pagan religions held a trinity, then the doctrine, in any form, is necessarily false. He assumes that if pagans hold a doctrine, it can have no truth in it. This assumption is fraught with theological and historical difficulties. In the past century, scholars have found four major early records which preserve accounts similar to the record of Genesis 1–11. The Epic of Gilgamesh, the Summerian King-List, the Semitic Old-Bablylonian Epic of Atrakhasis, and the Summerian Flood Story, all were written between the twentieth and seventeenth centuries B.C. Yet they all match the outline of Genesis 1–11. Each includes creation (except Gilgamesh), plus:

> 1. Divine decision to send a punishing flood; 2. One chosen man told to save self, family and creatures by building a boat; 3. A great flood destroys the rest of the people; 4. The boat grounds on a mountain; 5. Birds are sent forth to determine availability of habitable land; 6. The hero sacrifices to deity; 7. Renewal of mankind upon earth.[28]

One hundred years ago it was fashionable for theologians in higher-critical circles to insist that Genesis plagiarized these other Mesopotamian sources. Since then, it has become evident that they all independently record what they believed was a genuine event in ancient (to them as well as to us today) history.[29] It may well be also that the shades of trinities in pagan religions were not pagan creations which the Christian church wrongly adopted. Perhaps, instead, pagan religions retain "at least some hint of the truth," as C. S. Lewis put it,[30] which truth (perhaps) includes trinitarianism.

Wierwille neglects to note important distinctions between trinitarianism in Chris-

---

28. K. A. Kitchen, *The Bible in Its World* (Downers Grove, Ill.: InterVarsity, 1977), pp. 28, 29.

29. Cf. ibid., pp. 26-36, for a full description of these and other sources and their relationships to Genesis 1-11.

30. C. S. Lewis, "Answers to Questions on Christianity," in *God in the Dock* (Grand Rapids: Eerdmans, 1970), p. 54.

tianity and the "trinities" of paganism. J. L. Williams notes these differences:

> The Hindus, Greeks, and Romans had a three-god triad, but those did not come close to the Christian doctrine of the Trinity. Those cultures and religions had a three-god concept, but the members of their divine triads were not co-equal and co-eternal. Neither did they share the same nature and essence. They also did not have a perfect unity among them. In fact, the opposite was true.[31]

These religions may be called tritheistic, or, more accurately, polytheistic, but not trinitarian. They did not have one God of three persons, nor even three gods. Rather they had scores of gods of different strengths in constant conflict.

Noted historian Philip Schaff condemns the opinion that the doctrine of the Trinity originated in paganism:

> The Socinian and rationalistic opinion, that the church doctrine of the Trinity sprang from Platonism and Neo-Platonism is therefore radically false. The Indian Trimurti, altogether pantheistic in spirit, is still further from the Christian Trinity.[32]

Yet, Schaff recognizes some influence that Greek pagan thought had on Christian doctrine. That influence, he shows, was clearly not on the origin of Christian teachings, but on their *form*. This had to do especially with the words that early church leaders used to express the great truths:

> Only thus much is true, that the Hellenistic philosophy operated from without, as a stimulating force, upon the form of the whole patristic theology, the doctrines of the Logos and the Trinity among the rest; and that the deeper minds of heathen antiquity showed a presentiment of a threefold distinction in the divine essence; but only a remote and vague presentiment which, like all the deeper instincts of the heathen mind, serves to strengthen Christian truth. Far clearer and more fruitful suggestions presented themselves in the Old Testament. . . .[33]

Scholars have always recognized Greek influence not on Christian teaching, but on its "mental cast," its "phraseology and ideas"[34] as the *New Catholic Encyclopedia* puts it. The early church was at times driven to Greek philosophy (which was written in their native tongue) for technical terms to make clear the difference between valid Christian teaching and heretical perversions of Christian teaching.[35] This Greek influence had both positive and negative aspects, though the former has had the more lasting influence.

---

31. J. L. Williams, *Victor Paul Wierwille and The Way International* (Chicago: Moody, 1979), p. 78.

32. Philip Schaff, *History of the Christian Church* (New York: Scribner's, 1924), vol. 2, p. 566.

33. Ibid., pp. 566, 567.

34. *New Catholic Encyclopedia*, 14:58.

35. Ibid., p. 59.

Wierwille sums up his most critical argument when he writes that church leaders:

> . . . spoke of the Father as supreme, the true and only God, as without beginning, invisible, unbegotten and as such immutable; and the Son as inferior, and, as a real person, having a beginning, visible, begotten and mutable.[36]

Much of Wierwille's above statement is valid—leaders did see the Father as the true and only God, and the Son as a real person, who was visible. However, they did not all speak of the Son as inferior, nor did they think it was contradictory to consider Jesus to be simultaneously God and man. Wierwille considers it impossible for Jesus to be God, because he had the body of a man. The church felt the tension of saying Jesus was God and man at the same time, but thought Holy Scripture left no alternative but to accept this scriptural paradox.

Church leaders wrote different things concerning the Son of God. Some held him to be inferior to God. Some individuals even seem to write contrasting things about him. One can see why some variance would exist then. None of the early authors ever made the effort to *systematize* Christian thinking, and so stressed different aspects of their faith to address different situations. Plus, then, as today, different Christians had different depths of understanding which reflected the length of time they were Christian, their teachers, and the availability of all the books of Scripture.

Many of the leaders (contrary to Wierwille's claim) understood "the Father" to be the Godhead in general. As such they accepted the Son as fully divine and in no way inferior, except that for a time he took on humanity in order to live in the flesh among men. Some of the statements of church leaders which describe our Lord's divinity follow.

Ignatius was an early church father who was a disciple of Polycarp, and possibly of the apostle John. About A.D. 110 he wrote to the Romans "according to the love of Jesus Christ, our God . . ." (address). To the Ephesians he wrote, "For our God, Jesus the Christ, was conceived in the womb by Mary . . . " (18:2), and again,

> There is one Physician, who is both flesh and spirit, born and yet not born, who is God in man, true life in death, both of Mary and of God, first passible and then inpassible, Jesus Christ our Lord (7:2).

Ignatius also exhorts the Trallians to "continue in intimate union with Jesus Christ our God " (7:1).[37] Slightly later, about A.D. 125, an anonymous father wrote, "he sent him [Jesus] as God, he sent him as Man to men" (*Letter to Diognetus,* 7).

---

36. Wierwille, *Jesus Christ is Not God,* pp. 12, 13.

37. Many of Ignatius' Epistles have been printed in Syriac (Eastern Aramaic-Middle) as well as Greek, and much debate has ensued over whether the Greek or Syriac versions are the originals. The following references in the Syriac version also speak of the deity of Christ: *Trallians,* 6; *Smyrnaeans,* 5; *Ephesians,* 15.

Justin Martyr, who often seems to place Jesus below the Father, also speaks of him as God. In his *First Apology* (A.D. 140) he writes of the Son, "who also, being the first-begotten Word of God, is even God" (63). Later, in his *Dialogue with Trypho the Jew*, he notes that "He preexisted as the Son of the Creator of all things, being God, and that he was born a man by the virgin" (48) and so is "deserving to be worshipped, as God and as Christ" (63). Also, in *Against Praxeas*, he states that Jesus is "both man and God" (2).

Many other writers also spoke of Jesus' divinity. Tatian the Syrian, in his *Address to the Greeks* (ca. A.D. 165–175), claims, "We are not playing the fool, you Greeks, nor do we talk nonsense, when we report that God was born in the form of a man" (21). Irenaeus asserts the same in *Against Heresies* and cites the prophets as his authority (A.D. 180–199):

> He is Himself in his own right God and Lord and Eternal King and Only-begotten and Incarnate Word, proclaimed as such by all the Prophets (3, 19, 1).

Many writers in the following century made similar statements to describe that Jesus Christ is God as well as man. Unfortunately, there is no room here to include them all in full, though a list of many of these is cited below.[38]

Wierwille argues that church leaders did not speak of the Trinity until late. He further claims that the trinitarian formula found in Matthew 28:19 was not in the autograph, nor was it a part of Matthew until the fourth century:

> All extant Manuscripts do contain this verse in Matthew 28, the oldest from the fourth century during which trinitarianism was becoming a part of formal doctrine and writing. It would not have been difficult for scribes to insert "in the name of the Father, and of the Son, and the Holy Ghost," in place of the original "in my name." This must have been what happened because earlier manuscripts which Eusebius (who died in 340 A.D.) quoted in the early part of the fourth century could not have used the trinitarian formula. He cites Matthew 28:19 eighteen times without *once* using them. Rather, he wrote, ". . . baptizing them in my name."[39]

This claim of Wierwille is quite inaccurate. First, the 18 quotes in Eusebius never use the word "baptizing," either, so he is not describing a baptismal formula. Second, Eusebius did use the trinitarian words at least four times, a fact about which Wierwille is apparently ignorant.[40] It is very clear that Matthew 28:19 is a genuine part of the

---

38. Tertullian: *The Soul* (A.D. 208–212), 41, 3; *Against Praxeas* (A.D. 213), 13, 5; Hippolytus of Rome: *Refutation of all Heresies* (post A.D. 222), 10, 34; Clement of Alexandria: *Exhortation to the Greeks* (ante A.D. 200), 1, 7, 1; 10, 110, 1; Origen: *The Fundamental Doctrines* (A.D. 220–230), 1, Preface, 4; 4, 1, 6; Cyprian of Carthage: *Letter to Jubaianus* (A.D. 254–256), 73, 12; Lactanius: *The Divine Institutions* (A.D. 304–310), 4, 13, 1. Note that these authors represent a variety of backgrounds and homelands.

39. Wierwille, *Jesus Christ is Not God,*, pp. 19-20.

40. These are found in Eusebius' *Contra Marcellum* (twice), in *De Ecclesiastica Theologia,* and in a letter written to the church at Caesarea.

75

apostle's Gospel.[41] Wierwille's argument is almost entirely from silence. In addition, the trinitarian formula of Matthew 28:19 has been quoted many times by the early fathers, the references of which we cite below.[42] Many Fathers also reveal a strong belief in the Trinity, dating from the time of the apostles and shortly thereafter. Tertullian and those after him make efforts to describe in finer detail the three persons and the unity of the Godhead.[43]

In the early centuries of Christianity, a number of heresies were introduced into the church, but condemned by it. By looking at what was condemned by the church, we get an idea of what they believed about the person of Jesus Christ. Docetism was a trend which taught that Jesus did not suffer, he only appeared to suffer. "If he suffered he was not God; if he was God he did not suffer."[44] The church insisted Christ did really suffer. Yet, it did not refute the belief that, although he could suffer, he was God as well as man.

The church also rejected Gnosticism, types of which were taught by Saturnlius (c. A.D. 120), Basilides (c. A.D. 130), Cerinthus (late first century A.D.), and Marcion (c. A.D. 160). Teachings varied, but Jesus was usually a man empowered by God, or likely a man in appearance, or a being greater than man but less than God.[45]

Also condemned was Monarchianism in two forms. The first, Adoptionist or Dynamic Monarchianism, is very similar to Wierwille's doctrine. Its teachers, such as Theodotus, Artemon, and Paul of Samosata, "maintained that Jesus is God only in the sense that a power or influence from the Father rested upon His human person."[46] The church rejected this, reinforcing the long-held teaching that Jesus is more than a divinely begotten, commissioned, and empowered man. The second form of Monarchianism was Sabellianism. Although the church condemned its teaching that

41. For a full discussion of the Eusebian quotation and the text of Matthew 28:19, see Douglas Morton, "Ancient Heresies Modernized," *The Journal of Pastoral Practice* IV, 1:78-81.

42. *The Didache* (Palestine, A.D. 80), 7; Ignatius (of Antioch): *Epistle to the Philadelphians* (A.D. 110), Syriac 9; Justin Martyr (b. Samaria): *First Apology* (A.D.140), 61; Irenaeus (bishop of Lyons): *Against Heresies* (A.D. 180–199), bk. III, 17; Tertullian (of Carthage): *On Baptism* (A.D. 198–200), 13; *On Prescription Against Heretics* (A.D. 200), 20; Hippolytus: *Against Noetus* (A.D. 200–230), 14; (anonymous African?): *Against the Heretic Novatian* (A.D. 254–256), 3; Cyprian (bishop of Carthage): *The Seventh Council of Carthage* (A.D. 258), twice; (anonymous): *On Re-Baptism* (post A.D. 255?), 7; Gregory Thaumaturgus (bishop of Neocaesarea in Pontus): *A Sectional Confession of Faith* (A.D. 250–270), 13; (anonymous): *Constitutions of the Holy Apostles* (sections 3rd century A.D.), bk. II, 26; VI, 15; VII, 22; 40.

43. For examples see J. N. D. Kelly, *Early Christian Doctrines*, 2nd ed. (New York: Harper & Row, 1960), pp. 83-137, and William A. Jurgens, *The Faith of the Early Fathers* (Collegeville, Minn.: Liturgical Press, 1970), passim.

44. Bettenson, op. cit, p. 50.

45. Ibid., pp. 50-53.

46. F. L. Cross, E. A. Livingstone, ed., *The Oxford Dictionary of the Christian Church*, 2nd ed. (New York: Oxford University, 1974), p. 929.

the Father, Son, and Spirit were only modes of the Godhead, it did not condemn any emphasis on the deity of the Son. Finally, the church also condemned what is perhaps the ultimate slander against the person of the God-man Jesus Christ—Arianism. Even though many bishops at the Council of Nicea disliked the critical word "homoousios," they accepted the condemnation of Arius as valid and "Homoousios" as the one sound, though extra-scriptural, test which could discern ecclesiastical heretics.[47] Evidently the church was trying to keep a balance. It did not want to lift humanity from Jesus Christ. However, it did not want to be robbed of the revealed divinity of Christ, either.

When Did Trinitarianism Become Doctrine?

Here we take up the third primary argument presented in "The Origin of the Three-in-One God," the view of doctrinal development. Wierwille's underlying presumption is that, since there is some evidence of development of Christian doctrine regarding the Trinity, trinitarianism must have been created by the church and substituted for the original non-trinitarian monotheism. Wierwille quotes a section of the *New Catholic Encyclopedia* to support his premise. In it, he initially seems to have caught the Catholics red-handed in an admission that trinitarianism was not an apostolic teaching, but rather "became part of Christian doctrine in the fourth, not the first, century"[48]:

> It is difficult, in the second half of the 20th century, to offer a clear, objective and straightforward account of the revelation, doctrinal evolution, and theological elaboration of the mystery of the Trinity. . . .
>
> There is . . . recognition on the part of historians of dogma and systematic theologians that when one does speak of an unqualified Trinitarianism, one has moved from the period of Christian origins to, say, the last quadrant of the 4th century. It was only then that what might be called the definitive Trinitarian dogma "one God in three Persons" became thoroughly assimilated into Christian life and thought.
>
> . . . The dogmatic formula "one God in three Persons" . . . was the product of 3 centuries of doctrinal development.[49]

Wierwille misses the author's key, contrasting words. He asserts the authority for trinitarianism is God by calling it "revelation" in the opening sentence above, which Wierwille apparently overlooks. The *Encyclopedia* then contrasts the "theological elaboration" and "dogmatic formula" which later described and detailed the truth of the Trinity. The idea of the Trinity was not developed over the centuries, since the triune God always was and always will be. However, man's understanding and

---

47. *Encyclopedia Britannica* (New York: Encyclopedia Britannica, 1969), 3:634.
48. Wierwille, *Jesus Christ is Not God,* p. 13.
49. *New Catholic Encyclopedia* (New York: McGraw-Hill, 1967), p. 295, in Wierwille, *Jesus Christ is Not God,* p. 14.

theological expression or formula took time to develop as Christians explored the Scriptures and learned to express their faith in clear definitions. Later the same *Encyclopedia* article emphasizes that trinitarianism in its "strict," theological sense underwent development, while faith in the Trinity always existed in the church:

> If it is clear on one side that the dogma of the Trinity in the stricter sense of the word was a late arrival, product of 3 centuries' reflection and debate, it is just as clear on the opposite side that confession of the Father, Son, and Holy Spirit—and hence an elemental Trinitarianism—went back to the period of Christian origins.[50]

"Elemental Trinitarianism" is still trinitarianism like that of the fourth century, only the church had not thought out the implications of the belief and learned to describe it in detail.

Other articles in the *New Catholic Encyclopedia* detail the difference between the basic belief, or dogma, in the loose sense, and its theology, or elaboration. The opening paragraph of the article, "Development of Doctrine," explains:

> . . . the development of dogma is closely connected with the development of theology (the first is usually elaborated in the second). . . .[51]

The article on "Theology" reinforces this distinction:

> Since then [Aquinas] the term as used by Christians of their doctrine has meant the methodical elaboration of the truths of divine revelation by reason enlightened by faith. . . .[52]

Did the Roman Catholic Church (and Christianity at large) "create" trinitarianism, or plagiarize from paganism? No! Did the Christian church require time to put the pieces of revelation together, understand their relationship, and spell it out in understandable, discerning ways? Yes! Although trinitarianism was not in elaborate theological formulas in the first century, the New Testament and the primitive church did believe and teach it. J. N. Kelly describes this beginning phase of Christianity and the later elaboration:

> The ideas implicit in these early catechetical and liturgical formulae, as in the New Testament writers' use of the same dyadic and triadic patterns, represent a pre-reflective, pre-theological phase of Christian belief. It was out of the raw material thus provided by the preaching, worshipping Church that theologians had to construct their more sophisticated accounts of the Christian doctrine of the Godhead.[53]

Gerald O'Collins calls the "elemental trinitarianism" of the Scriptures, its "trini-

---

50. *New Catholic Encyclopedia*, 14:300.
51. Ibid., 4:940.
52. Ibid., 14:39.
53. Kelly, op. cit., p. 90.

tarian face" and notes the "trinitarian shapp" of Christian experience.[54]

The early church for a time was in a quandry over how to handle the totality of scriptural revelation. It saw in Scripture the deity of the Son and the Spirit, and yet knew only one God. What were they to do? Were they to reject the passages that taught the deity of the Son and Spirit, or were they to try to eliminate their monotheistic heritage? Actually, they did neither; instead, they rightly synthesized what seemed paradoxical. Schaff explains:

> The unity of God was already immovably fixed by the Old Testament as a fundamental article of revealed religion in opposition to all forms of idolatry. But the New Testament and the Christian consciousness as firmly demanded faith in the divinity of the Son, who effected redemption, and of the Holy Spirit, who founded the church and dwells in believers; and these apparently contradictory interests could be reconciled only in the form of the Trinity; that is, by distinguishing in the one and indivisible essence of God three hypostases or persons; at the same time allowing for the insufficiency of all human conceptions and words to describe such as unfathomable mystery.[55]

In the beginning centuries of Christianity, as now, some groups and individuals refused the synthesis that the church fathers detail in the opening centuries of the Christian era:

> From the logical point of view, it could probably be said that the heresies of this time (perhaps of any time?) have as a common note oversimplification: the selection of a single alternative in despair of synthesis. Arianism was no exception.[56]

The trinitarian *formula*, then, was not foreign to Scripture and apostolic teaching. Rather, it brought together and spelled out beliefs long held in some form:

> "One God in three Persons" was simply a restatement, a legitimately condensed and compact version of the more loosely organized NT teaching. Key texts were cited in support. . . .[57]

Why were these restatements necessary? If trinitarianism is not a pagan importation, then why did the NT not enunciate it in detail while later Christianity did? The *New Catholic Encyclopedia* outlines the primary impetus:

> In the golden age of the Fathers, the elaboration of theology was stimulated mainly by the need to rectify misconceptions of the faith and to oppose Trinitarian and Christological errors.[58]

A section of the *Encyclopedia's* article, "Dogma," sums up the Christian approach to theological development:

---

54. Gerald O'Collins, "The Trinity: 3 x 1 = 1," *U.S. Catholic*, Feb. 1981, p. 7.
55. Schaff, op. cit., 2:566.
56. *New Catholic Encyclopedia*, 14:297.
57. Ibid., p. 299.
58. Ibid., p. 50.

. . . in enunciating a new dogma the Church does not add to revelation but simply declares or defines what has been revealed. The Church's task is to guard the deposit of faith; this involves expounding it to different ages so that it always remains a living thing. The Church does not create a new thing; it merely states what has been revealed.[59]

Conclusion

In all, "The Origin of the Three-in-One God" reveals either a measure of ignorance, or manipulation of the facts of Christian church history, or both. Documentation is lacking on some important points, and at times the chapter sadly misinterprets the true situation. Often sources are cited to reinforce Wierwille's points that in reality militate against them. Christian trinitarianism does not find its origin in pagan triads, but in Christian wrestlings with revelation.[60] The early church then, as the orthodox church today, understood the presence of the humanity of Christ, but at the same time lauded his divinity. Wierwille apparently lacks understanding of doctrinal development and of the distinctions between faith and dogma, theology, doctrine and formulae. These elements exist in the doctrinal history of every religious group, The Way International included.

One argument in "The Origin of the Three-in-One God" which this paper was not able to take up is the issue of the purpose, mechanics, and outcome of the Council of Nicea in A.D. 325. Wierwille asserts that this council was but the tool of Constantine, which he used "to legitimatize his position" at which he "used his political power" to bring about the verdict,[61] against the true inclination of the bishops in attendance. But it should be noted that he wrongly claims that the bishops were from the Occident. This makes the decision appear lopsided. Wierwille's argument could be refuted in detail. The doctrinal development, the hesitation of many at the word *homoousios* (not the doctrinal concept), the political machinations of the Arians after Nicea, doctrinal understanding after Nicea and the Council of Constantinople (which the deceased Constantine could not have ramrodded even if he wanted to) are just a few insights into the validity of the Nicean formula.

Overall, this chapter of *Jesus is not God* falls far short of being an accurate, reliable treatment of the actual "Origin of the Three-in-One God," which is His own existence revealed to man in holy Scripture and made progressively more understandable to the Christian church throughout the centuries by the Holy Spirit.

ADDENDUM

Not only does it seem that Wierwille manipulates early church history, but it seems that he also attempts to manipulate later church history. He claims that not only early

59. Ibid., 4:948.
60. For a further discussion of this, see Christopher Kaiser, "The Ontological Trinity in the Context of Historical Religions," *Scottish Journal of Theology* 29:301-310.
61. Wierwille, *Jesus Christ is not God*, p. 23.

church leaders were on "his side," but also that later church leaders were with him. As an example, he cites Luther. To him, Luther was as anti-trinitarian as he is, but was afraid to assert it. As evidence of Luther's anti-trinitarian stance, he cites Storr and Flatt's work:

> Storey [sic] and Flatt's Biblical Theology, 2d edition, page 301, states regarding the words three persons, etc. . . . "Among the advocates for their expulsion . . . were a number of the first divines of the age, not excepting Munnis and even Luther himself.—Yet, to prevent the charge of Arianism or Socinianism, which he (Luther) knew his enemies would eagerly seize the least pretext to prefer against them, Luther yielded to Melanchthon's wishes, and in the Augsburg Confession, the doctrine of the trinity is couched in the old Scholastic terms."
>
> This indicates clearly that Luther and other men of the Reformation period did not put the trinity into the creed because they believed it to be true, but in order to escape the charge of heresy which was labeled against Arius and Socinius. I'm surprised by the great man's actions, but that is man.[62]

Parts of the above are annoying, such as Wierwille's misspelling of Storr's name, and the minor misquote in the addition of the word "were." But the most disturbing aspect of Wierwille's use of Storr is his complete misunderstanding (or misrepresentation) of Storr's words. A closer look at Storr's words reveals that Luther did not disagree with the Trinity, but was afraid of the *words*, or theological terminology such as the Latin word "person" (*persona*), which might imply tritheism instead of trinitarianism. Note this larger quotation from the same part of Storr:

> On the words *persona*, (etc.). . . . Much has been said, about the time of the Reformation, concerning the tendency of these terms to lead to tritheism; and among the advocates for their expulsion from theological disquisition, might be mentioned a number of the first divines of the age, not excepting Minnius and even Luther himself.—Yet, to prevent the charge of Arianism or Socinianism, which he knew his enemies would eagerly seize the least pretext to prefer against them, Luther yielded to Melanchthon's wishes, and in the Augsburg Confession, the doctrine of the Trinity is couched in the old scholastic terms.
>
> On this subject, the sentiments of the ablest divines of the present day have been thus expressed by the Rev. Dr. Miller: "We found it in use; and not knowing a better term for the purpose intended, we have cheerfully adopted and continue to use it still. We by no means understand it, however, in a gross or carnal sense."[63]

It is clear that in context Luther and the other theologians believed fully in the Trinity. In fact, they were so concerned to keep the doctrine sound that they searched for proper terms to express it that would not lean to tritheism.

---

62. Victor Paul Wierwille, "Forgers of the Word," *Bibliography—Jesus Christ is not God* (New Knoxville, Ohio: American Christian Press, n.d.), p. 23.

63. G. C. Storr & Flatt, *Biblical Theology*, S. S. Schmucker, trans., 2nd ed. (New York: Griffin, Wilcox & Co., 1836), p. 301.

Although Luther strove throughout his life for accurate theological expression of revealed truths, he apparently always thought that the Latin "person" (*persona*) was the best word available to express trinitarian truth. In 1537, over 17 years *after* the Augsburg Confession was written, and over 15 years *after* Luther had been censured as heretical, excommunicated by the pope and banned by the emperor, he proclaimed his personal faith in the Trinity in Part I of the *Smalcald Articles*. Although he had already been condemned as worse or as bad as Arius and Socinius, he still opted for the Latin "person" (*persona,* or *personae* in the plural):

I. (English)	I. (Latin)
That Father, Son, and Holy Ghost, three distinct persons in one divine essence and nature are one God, who has created heaven and earth.[64]	Pater, Filius et Spiritus Sanctus, in una divina essentia et natura, tres distinctae personae, sunt unus Deus, qui creavit coelum et terram.

---

64. *Triglot Concordia* (St. Louis: Concordia Publishing House, 1921).

The Alberto Phenomenon

A Special Report by Kurt Goedelman

The Lord Jesus Christ, the Sovereign over the church, commended the church at Ephesus because they tried those "which say they are apostles, and are not, and hast found them liars" (Rev. 2:2). Ever since the founding of the early church, men have made false religious claims. These religious opportunists, whether from a desire for fame or fortune, have at times sought followers from among God's people. The Savior, who hates falsehood and sham, expects his people to test the claims of men who seek to influence His church, and if their claims do not stand up, they must be exposed for the deception they have practiced.

A Sinister Plot?

One such questionable claimant was John Todd, a professed ex-grand Druid who was thrust into national notoriety by Jack Chick's comic-book publications of *Angel of Light* and *Spellbound*. It seems as though the sensationalism of these Chick Publications had hardly died away before an even more startling Chick publication rolled from the presses. These are two booklets entitled *Alberto* and *Double Cross*. Chick Publications states that these comics are based on the experiences of Dr. Alberto Rivera and that the accounts in *Alberto* and *Double Cross* are true.[1]

Rivera, a Spaniard, describes himself as a former Jesuit priest, a bishop, and a secret agent of the Catholic Church whose mission was to infiltrate and destroy Protestant denominations. He claims that in Spain alone he helped destroy at least 19 churches by discrediting, isolating, or murdering the pastors of the churches.[2] In addition, these publications announce many other undocumented accusations which include: homosexuality abounding through the Roman Catholic system from priests to cardinals;[3] Lincoln's assassination was a Catholic plot;[4] Katherine Kuhlman, the late faith healer, was a Vatican agent sent to destroy the Charismatic Renewal in the United States from within;[5] Jim Jones, author of the 1978 Jonestown mass-murder in

---

1. Letter from Antichrist Information Center (Rivera's current organization) dated January 30, 1980, which is distributed by Chick Publications.
2. *Alberto*, pp. 20, 22.
3. Ibid., p. 12.
4. Father Chinique, *50 Years in the "Church" of Rome*, p. 512.
5. *Double Cross*, pp. 27, 28.

Guyana, was a Jesuit;[6] 86 percent of the Catholic priesthood are undergoing psychological and psychiatric treatments;[7] the pope is not the true head of the Catholic Church, but rather the highest ranking Jesuit, who, according to Rivera, is called the "black Pope,"[8] and the name of every Protestant is currently being recorded by a computer located in the Vatican.[9]

To challenge the falsehood of such statements, *Our Sunday Visitor*, a Catholic publication, has offered a $10,000 reward to anyone for proof of many of Alberto's claims.[10]

Although Chick Publications has gone to great expense to promote these booklets, many Christian organizations have not been swayed by Chick and have openly come out against such unsupported attacks on Catholicism. Two such Protestant challengers are the Reverend Grady Cothen, speaking on behalf of the Southern Baptist Sunday School Board, and Dan Penwell, marketing director of Zondervan Publishing Company, who announced that Zondervan Bookstores have been advised that *Alberto* is unsuitable for distribution.

Chick has countered these moves by publishing a tract entitled *My Name? . . . In The Vatican?*. In that publication it is claimed that the Vatican is behind the Christian bookstores' refusal to sell his publications. Accusations are further made that the Catholic system has organized "set-up" customers who are actually members of the Legion of Mary or from the Catholic Youth Action, who create trouble within the bookstores who sell these publications by claiming that they will boycott the stores. Further, he implies that there are only a few gospel bookstores that have not given in to Rome and of course, as expected, these stores are the ones who will continue to push Chick's *Alberto* publications. We are told that they do this because they see *Alberto* as the *only effective soul winning book* to win Catholics that's published today (emphasis added).[11]

Chick Publications, in its commitment to the *Alberto* story, has sent form letters to those inquiring about the *Alberto* matter in which they offer to supply Christians with free copies of the tract, *My Name? . . . In The Vatican?*, to distribute to each member of their church in an effort to publicize the Alberto saga.

Examining the Claims

But what of the many claims made by Dr. Rivera? Are they true? Can they be believed? Is the Roman Catholic Church trying to take over? Mr. Chick offset any

---

6. Ibid., p. 30.
7. *Alberto*, p. 10.
8. Ibid., pp. 9, 10, 28.
9. Ibid., p. 20.
10. *Our Sunday Visitor*, March 1, 1981.
11. *My Name? . . . In the Vatican?* p. 17. However, it is interesting to note that in later editions of this tract the quote has been changed to read: ". . . because they see it is *one of the best* soul winning books to win Catholics that's published today" (emphasis added).

claims of fraud that might be lodged against Alberto by issuing a letter in which he announced that his office received a telephone call from a European reporter telling of a sweep being made by priests throughout Spain destroying all evidence that Dr. Rivera ever existed. This approach may seem familiar to many, as it is identical with the position adopted by John Todd in which he stated that his records were also destroyed.[12] The only difference is that Todd's records were supposed to have been destroyed by the Illuminati, while Rivera's documents are said to have been removed by the Catholic system.

In recent articles by Gary Metz, which were published in *Christianity Today*[13] and *Cornerstone*[14] magazines, Rivera's accounts of his life story are shown to be false. Metz documented that Rivera, also known as Alberto Romero, is a native of the Canary Islands. His travels as well as his association with Christian organizations are extensive. During the time he claimed to be a Jesuit priest in Spain he was in reality married to Carmen Lydia Torres and had been located in Hoboken, New Jersey, and El Paso, Texas. These facts also render inconsistent his claim to have been in Guatemala during the mid-sixties. In addition, Metz has uncovered the fact that Rivera had been charged with several counts of criminal activity. He fled New Jersey leaving numerous debts and a warrant for his arrest on charges of bad check writing. Florida warrants have also been issued for the theft of a Bank Americard credit card and for unauthorized use of an automobile. Additional evidence also shows he is currently involved in a court action in Southern California in which he is accused of fraud. His testimonies regarding his priestly activities lack any verification and are publicly denied by the Catholic Church. The claims of Rivera to have numerous degrees, including a Masters in psychology and at least three Doctorates, also lack any valid documentation.

Jack Chick, in an attempt to counter the material presented by Mr. Metz in the aforementioned articles, has sent a letter to bookstore owners. He announced that Rome has slammed at Chick Publications using writer Gary Metz. But Chick's rebuttal actually contains nothing more than vague objections, avoiding many of the main issues contained in Metz's articles. However, he does attempt to answer the charges of the Florida warrants by stating that two "Christian" brethren approached Dr. Rivera and offered their help in his ministry. Their help included the use of one man's credit card, while the other offered the use of his car. We are then asked to believe that when Rivera crossed the Florida state line these "Christian" brethren turned out to be Catholic plants and promptly reported the theft of their car and credit card by Alberto.

---

12. For more information on Todd and the Illuminati, see G. R. Fisher, "Doomsday Postponed," *The Journal of Pastoral Practice* III, 4:99-103.

13. *Christianity Today*, March 13, 1981:50-53.

14. *Cornerstone* 9, 53:29-31. This article has been reprinted in tract form and is available from CARIS, P.O. Box 1783, Santa Ana, CA 92702.

Chick also mentioned John Todd in his letter, claiming that *Christianity Today* similarly attacked John Todd's ministry, destroying it, but that the periodical has since issued a letter apologizing for all the errors contained in their article about him. Upon checking with *Christianity Today's* office it was learned that they never "issued a letter apologizing for all the errors" nor did they ever have any intention of retracting their story, or hear of an impending lawsuit by Todd, two additional claims made by Chick in his letter. Chick further claimed that Gary Metz called several times to Chick Publications seeking employment, but was turned down each time. It is then implied that possibly Metz's articles were an act of revenge. However, does this not contradict Chick's former statement in which he claimed that Gary Metz was used by Rome to slam Chick Publications? In addition, Gary Metz has denied the accusation made by Chick concerning his calling for employment.[15]

The latest effort to undercut the responses to *Alberto* and to promote further the sensational assertions of Rome's desire to take over the world have been released in a tract entitled *Kiss The Protestants Good-Bye*. In it we are given the definition of Protestants as those "people who used to know what is going on." Also unveiled is how the Roman Catholic institution has planned to do away with Bible-believing Protestants of the twentieth century. We are informed that Rome is behind the conflicting theories of prophecy, i.e., various views on the rapture and the millennium. Also that the Jesuits of Rome selected B. F. Westcott and F. J. Hort successfully to destroy the King James Bible by the use of Catholic manuscripts which, we are told, the Revised Version was based upon. Other claims along this line include the assertion that over 100 versions of the Bible which are currently on the market are all based on Roman Catholic manuscripts. Chick's deep commitment to the King James Version seems to agree with the current distortion that asserts that the translators were also inspired. An additional charge asserts that Catholics appeal to Christian bookstores to carry their (Catholic) material and then priests tell their parishioners when to go and buy from these bookstores.

Further, we are told that the secret sign, which was to be given to the Jesuits worldwide when the ecumenical movement had successfully wiped out Protestantism, consisted of the President of the United States taking his oath of office facing an obelisk,[16] just as the pope faces the obelisk in St. Peters Square in the Vatican. We are then informed that on January 20, 1981, Ronald Reagan faced the Washington Monument (an obelisk) during his swearing-in ceremony. So, according to Chick's (and Rivera's) claim, Protestantism has been successfully wiped out. It is interesting to note that in Chick's publication *Sabatoge* (copyrighted 1979) mention is made of

---

15. Private letter from Metz to author.

16. Webster's dictionary defines obelisk as a tall, slender, four-sided pillar gradually tapering as it rises, having the top in the form of a pyramid. Chick describes it as a symbol of Nimrod or Baal as God, also as a Masonic symbol (*Sabotage*, pp. 21, 30).

the obelisk in St. Peter's Square,[17] however, we are not informed of the upcoming sign of the successful annihilation of Protestantism. It is only after the inauguration had taken place on the west front of the Capitol that we were told of this secret sign, which was allegedly given to Alberto and other Jesuits more than 14 years ago. Is this not like prophesying President Reagan's attempted assassination on March 31, 1981?[18]

Misquotations also appear in this publication. For example, it is asserted that Fr. Juan Martin DeNicholas admits that the papers issued to Dr. Alberto Rivera were certificates of the archdiocese of Madred-Alcala. However, upon checking the quote by Fr. DeNicholas, one finds that he does not state that the papers were issued to Rivera but rather deals only with the year of date which appears on the certificate and observes that there was no Spanish Jesuit by the name of Rivera at that time. Other declarations announce that Dr. Scofield's version of the King James Bible was controlled by Rome. According to the tract, "Chick smelled a rat . . . a big one," one Sunday while attending a seminar exposing Masonry. Chick heard the speaker make a statement that Dr. Scofield was a good Mason. It was then, Chick claimed, that he knew he had been set up, having previously placed his trust in the Scofield version. It was then that the Lord moved and put Chick and Rivera together.

Conclusions

In summary, Jack Chick and his publishing company, which has served the cause of Christ so well in the past through their superb artistic talent, will be deeply hurt through the causes they have recently championed—first with Todd, now with Alberto Rivera. Chick states that no publisher would touch Rivera with a ten-foot pole because it would cost the publisher his business as well as his reputation. This is indeed what will happen to Chick publications if they do not check the credentials of those they back more carefully. His ministry in the past has been a very effective instrument for producing material which indeed has won many souls for the Lord Jesus Christ. Possibly it is because of the great effectiveness of his ministry that the Enemy of our souls would seek to destroy it. We can see in his recent publications a very judgmental attitude towards both Catholics and Protestants. His publications imply that Protestants who do not believe that the facts support his case are in fact siding with Satan. Those who know Christ savingly share Mr. Chick's concern for Catholics to come to know Jesus Christ as their personal Lord and Savior. However, his methods of reaching them through questionable and even false assertions must be challenged. The Catholic Church is now planning new moves against his publications and announced their intention to prosecute Chick for consumer frauds. Their mail fraud complaint against Chick Publications will be based on Chick's letters sent to

---

17. *Sabotage*, p. 30.
18. The assassination attempt on President Reagan's life took place March 30, 1981.

inquiring individuals and Christian bookstores asserting that the events in his publications are truthful accounts. Chick indeed stands to lose a great deal, and we as Christians will see a great talent stifled through hours of litigation. Believers need to pray earnestly for this Christian organization which has become enamored with questionable claimants like Alberto and John Todd. To become their defenders when the facts speak so strongly against them only succeeds in dividing the brethren. Like the church at Ephesus, we need to examine carefully the credentials of those who claim to present God's truth and, if we find them false, our faithfulness to that truth requires that we expose them.

NEWS NOTES

PENETRATING MORMONISM
IN NEW ZEALAND

A significant breakthrough to Mormons in New Zealand has recently come about through the conversion of Ronald and Roberta Rees. The couple had been Mormons for some 17 years and are in their early thirties. Nine years ago they established the first privately owned bookshop catering to supplying the LDS people of New Zealand with the church's book requirements. Their operation covered a block in size and included two stores, known as Beehive Books.

Because they carried older as well as more recent LDS books and took time to read many of the older publications, they became aware that teachings of the past were different from those of present-day Mormonism. In 1980 a non-Mormon customer drew their attention to the Tanners' work, *Mormonism: Shadow or Reality,* which they ordered from the States. Before that volume arrived they learned of the Tanners' *Changing World of Mormonism,* which Moody Press had published, and were able to obtain a copy of it from a local dealer in Christian books.

After reading *Changing World,* they decided to leave the church, in the process finding Christ as Savior. They were excommunicated in March of this year. They loaned the Tanners book to seven of their friends, and all decided to withdraw from the LDS Church. Since then they have ordered a huge amount of the Tanners' books, and as a result of their efforts nearly 70 persons have left the Mormon Church, most of whom have become Christians. Those who have been reached included a bishop, five returned missionaries, and two stake High Counselmen. An Ex-Mormons for Jesus group has been organized, and mailings have been sent to the entire bookstore Mormon mailing list, telling of their reasons for leaving the LDS Church. Every day letters and phone calls are received bringing new inquiries.

They are disposing of their LDS books and converting their large operation to a Christian bookstore ministry. Prayers are requested that this good work will be forwarded by the Lord. One returned LDS missionary, after being shown the contradictons in Mormonism, said with tears in his eyes, "I've wasted two years of my life and all that money for a lie." Two days later he accepted the Lord. He is now on the verge of converting his relatives, who are third generation Mormons.

NEW PHASE OF THE MOON

The Unification Church, known as the Moonies, has lost its libel suit against a British newspaper—a real setback for the followers of Rev. Moon. On the American scene, the news media are now reporting that Moon stands to lose his right to remain in the U.S.A. Here, reportedly, by virtue of his marriage to a woman who has been granted temporary privileges for residency in the U.S., Moon has been permitted to remain in the country, but that privilege is now under review. If further extension is not granted, both Moon and his wife will face deportation.

JW INTERNAL STRIFE

The Jehovah's Witnesses have faced some embarrassing losses in recent months. Several leading figures have broken with the Watchtower leadership, among them the nephew of the president Frederick Franz. Some, it is reported, claim a born-again experience. A number have complained of the autocratic rule exercised by the Brooklyn headquarters.

BOOK BRIEFS

William Lane Craig, *The Existence of God and the Beginning of the Universe*. San Bernardino, CA: Here's Life Publishers, Inc., 1979. 107pp. Available from the publishers, P.O. Box 1576, San Bernardino, CA 92402 (or from the author at Trinity Theological Seminary, Deerfield, IL 60015)—for $8.00.

This concise and clearly written publication by a professor at Trinity Theological Seminary in Chicago brings together the heart of his Ph.D. dissertation. Dr. Craig demonstrates both from philosophy and from the latest studies in the field of astronomy and physics that the universe necessarily had a beginning. Since some para-Christian groups, such as the Mormons, postulate the eternity of matter, and some Eastern cults teach the eternal existence of an impersonal life-force, pastors should be aware of the material in this potent volume that undercuts such positions.

Dr. Craig presents in simplified form two well-accepted philosophical propositions that demonstrate that "actual infinity" cannot exist in created reality. The impact of such logical arguments is that it is logically impossible for the universe to have existed infinitely.

Since, as Dr. Craig recognizes, the average person feels uncomfortable with and even distrusts philosophical arguments, he establishes the same point from the latest thinking in the scientific field. He shows that the current observable data in the field of astro-physics supports the expanding universe model and discredits the steady-state model (in which the universe is viewed as experiencing no change) as well as the oscillating model (in which the universe is viewed as eternally expanding and contracting). Since the expanding universe model requires that as one goes back in time he reaches the point in which the universe was "shrunk down to nothing at all" (as Hoyle expressed it), this means that at one time the universe did not exist. Dr. Craig presents these extremely difficult concepts with clarity and exceptionally pointed quotations from noted authorities in the field.

Having shown the philosophical and scientific evidence that requires one to conclude that the universe had a beginning, Dr. Craig weighs the options that such a beginning was either caused or uncaused. He presents statements from leading thinkers (who are not theists or Christian philosophers) who find it impossible to accept the proposition that something could come from nothing. Dr.Craig notes that even skeptical philosopher David Hume "admitted that it is preposterous to think anything could come into existence without a cause" (p. 83). With such concession made by nearly all philosophical schools, Dr. Craig is ready to turn to his final consideration of whether such a cause for the beginning of the universe would be personal or impersonal.

Dr. Craig's book is a stimulating piece of work, and the pastor who is looking for some usable illustrations and well-chosen quotations for a message to high school or college students will find his opening chapter alone worth the price of the book. In that chapter he shows the implications upon morals and values that must be accepted if God does not exist. Best of all, the work concludes with a practical chapter on how to come to a personal relationship with the God to whom the finite universe bears witness.

—W.P.W.

Maurice Barnett. *Mormonism Against Itself.* Cullman, AL: Printing Service, 1980. Volume I, 146pp, $9.00. Available from the publisher at 1822 Highland Drive, N.W., Cullman, AL 35055.

Pastor Barnett has added a helpful tool for pastors who are seeking to improve their witness to Mormons in their community. The tool consists almost entirely of photo-mechanical reproductions of Mormon materials in 8½" x 11" size, punched to fit in a three-ring binder (you supply the binder). This format enables the user to remove from the package (or binder) those pages and topics he wishes to use in his discussion with Mormons. It has the added advantage of enabling one who wishes to lecture on some aspect of Mormonism to assemble the pages as suits his presentation. The back of each page is blank and can be used to type the observations or the content one wishes to present before extracting a quotation from Mr. Barnett's material. Since the pages are loose-leafed, they can also be run through a Thermo Fax so that over-heads can be made. The over-heads can be inter-leafed right in between the pages and thus kept in order for presentation. The speaker can read from the printed copy while the audience watches the same material on the screen.

Pastor Barnett has spared no expense in obtaining the best possible copies of rare Mormon books and manuscripts that show the falseness and contradictoriness of Mormonism. Volume I covers the claims made by the Mormons, a consideration of the *Book of Mormon,* its changes and lack of support from archeology, Joseph Smith's revelations and the changes made in them, the prophet's failure to follow his own revelation (Word of Wisdom), and weakness of his First Vision story. A second volume is in preparation and will include Mormonism's prophetic failures, the Adam-God doctrine, Blood Atonement, etc. One would spend far more than the cost of this work to assemble such a collection. Highly recommended.—W.P.W.

FILMSTRIPS

Jehovah's Witness: The Christian View and *Mormonism: The Christian View*. Personal Freedom Outreach, P.O. Box 26062, St. Louis, MO 63136. Purchase $19.95 each. Phone (314) 388-2648.

These presentations include a wealth of illustrated knowledge on the Jehovah's Witnesses and the Mormons in the following areas: their histories; the major doctrines they teach; the programs by which converts are made and indoctrinated; extensive review of their internal difficulties, such as false prophecy, which show these religions to be of human, not divine, origin; and suggestions Christians may follow in witnessing to members of these pseudo-Christian religions. These filmstrips show these cults to be not only doctrinally radically different from Christianity, but internally corrupt as well.

Each filmstrip set includes a filmstrip of approximately 110 color frames and a 45 or 48 minute cassette narration boxed together for shelf storage. These frames include excellent color reproductions of all important historical sites, individuals and doctrinal excerpts from primary source books. Brochure outlines of the presentations are available at minor cost for distribution to viewers. Some important graphic improvements have been made since these presentations first appeared in 35 mm slide format. (Although the programs are still available in slide form for $50 and $60 respectively.)

The filmstrips were produced by Wesley P. Walters, well-known Christian researcher of Mormonism, and by M. Kurt Goedelman, whose tracts on the Witnesses are used internationally. The programs have received excellent reviews by such respected authors as Edmond Gruss, James Bjornstad, and William Cetnar. Not only is the price well within the reach of any parish, but the presentations have been enthusiastically received by every congregational group, including adult classes, youth, singles, couples' clubs, and Sunday School teachers. Some 80 percent of converts to the Witnesses and Mormons come from Christian denominational churches. This can be prevented by simple "vaccination"—and these filmstrips are the right tools for the job!—John Juedes

Preaching

JAY ADAMS
Editor

Audience Analysis
And Martyn Lloyd-Jones

ROBERT PENNY

Fellow preacher, may I ask a question: "Whom are you talking to?" In the context of the pulpit, "Whom are you preaching to?" Do you *know* the people for whom you are preparing and to whom you are preaching sermons?

That sermon preparation is one of the most practical aspects of the pastoral ministry, surely none of us will doubt. Understand, then, that the matter of audience analysis, or if you prefer, congregational or pew analysis, is a phase of sermon preparation, a prelude. Concurrently with sermon preparation, it must be going on all the time.

It may interest you to know that of the many who are speaking on this increasingly discussed topic, a Reformed preacher of note has set forth some principles. The late Dr. Martyn Lloyd-Jones, formerly preacher of Westminster Chapel, London, has spoken to preachers and students on this subject.

Introductory

A major area of concern for Lloyd-Jones is his view of the listeners of preaching. It must be acknowledged that his major element does *partake* of the matter of the fundamental elements of a sermon, as well as preparation and delivery of sermon. It does, however, deserve a separate discussion because: (1) Lloyd-Jones isolated it and treated it as a matter towards which the first three matters are directed and bent, and (2) he believed that it, to some extent at least, regulated the first three matters.

Under this major area of concern, one can see features of sensitivity to a basic presupposition of modern communications theory and to its early finding concerning the four basic elements.[1] The basic presupposition is that communication, including speaker audience or preacher congregation, is a *process*.[2] The matters of the fundamental elements of a sermon and its preparation actually embrace what modern communication research has found to be two of the basic elements of the communications process, the *source* and the *message*. Both of these are basic to any communica-

---

1. Cf. David K. Berlo, *The Process of Communication: An Introduction to Theory and Practice* (New York: Holt, Rinehart and Winston, 1960), pp. 40-72.

2. Cf. Raymond McLaughlin, *Communication for the Church* (Grand Rapids: Zondervan, 1968), p. 62.

tion. The same may be said of the elements of the *channel* and the *receiver*. The following discussion will reveal Lloyd-Jones's awareness of and sensitivity to the dynamics which operate in these two basic elements. It must be acknowledged that he never used these terms nor does he demonstrate any familiarity with any formal studies in modern communications theory or findings. He does, nevertheless, seem to have thought and operated within the confines of its principles or laws, which are now being brought to light in recent scientific and empirical studies.[3]

In this discussion we will explore his general views of the necessity of receiver-congregation awareness, his views of audience analysis, and his views of message delivery in the light of rudimentary factors of receiver-congregation awareness.

General Views of Audience Awareness

Lloyd-Jones believed it to be "equally essential" that the preacher "should look" at the "people who are listening" to him. He called this the "question of the relationship" between "the pew and the pulpit," and by the length of his discussion alone relating to "the people in the pew," he demonstrated his sensitivity for the receiver-congregation. "After all," said Lloyd-Jones, "[the preacher] is preaching to them." He went on to reveal an awareness of the difference between expressive communication and rhetorical communication. He reminded the preacher that he "is not just standing there to voice certain of his own ideas and opinions." That would be mere *expressive* communication. But the preacher's purpose is a *rhetorical* one. Lloyd-Jones elaborated: "[The preacher] is there, primarily, to address people who have come together in order to listen to him and to what he has to say."[4]

Lloyd-Jones deplored a problem of the past which reflected an insensitivity on the part of some preachers in this area. He saw it as a "tendency" for the "pulpit to be almost independent of the pew." There was, on the other hand, a tendency for the

---

3. Cf. Baumann, who gives the warning that it seems "unwise for the preacher to shut his mind to the findings and insights of the communications theorists. The man who is called by God to preach the Gospel ought to concern himself with gaining more proficiency in his task. Any useful insights ought to be incorporated into the service of Christ and his Church." J. D. Baumann, *An Introduction to Contemporary Preaching* (Grand Rapids: Baker, 1972), p. 21. Cf. also G. Doyle Wright, who discussed as a major element in Augustine's preaching theory "the accommodation of different styles to meet different needs in the congregation" and how Augustine "sought to conform his sermons to the needs and capacities of his hearers." "Augustine's Sermonic Method," *Westminster Theological Journal* 39 (Spring 1977):235.

4. Lloyd-Jones, *Preaching and Preachers* (Grand Rapids: Zondervan, 1972), p. 121. Cf. McCroskey, who said, "expressive communication is source-centered, whereas rhetorical communication is receiver-centered." J. C. McCroskey, *An Introduction to Rhetorical Communication*, 2nd ed. (Englewood Cliffs: Prentice-Hall, Inc., 1972), p. 34. Cf. also Karl Barth's comments, which suggest the benefits here of a warm, pastoral approach to the people. *The Preaching of the Gospel*, trans. B. E. Hooke (Philadelphia: Westminster Press, 1963). Cf. also Richard H. Lueke, "Renaissance Rhetoric and Born Again Preaching," *Theology Today* 35 (December 1978):168-77.

"pew to revere the preacher sometimes almost to the point of idolatry." Whatever may be said as to the priority of cause and effect in this relationship, the result was unfortunate, as an illustration by Lloyd-Jones proves. He related that once a poor woman was leaving a service and was asked if she could follow the message. The woman replied, "Far be it from me to presume to understand such a great man as that!"[5]

But Lloyd-Jones did not lay the entire burden on the pulpit. With apparent approval he quoted one writer who said: "The world is dying for want, not of good preaching but of good hearing." His sensitivity to the receiver/congregation should not be taken as a suggestion for a wholesale capitulation to "modern man" and allowing what he can accept to become "the determining factor." He rejected all such "talk" about "modern man come of age." His negative views along these lines must be taken with this apparent sensitivity to the receiver/congregation.[6]

Lloyd-Jones's views on the definition and purpose of the sermon also demonstrate this receiver/congregation sensitivity:

> A sermon is not an essay and is not meant, primarily, for publication, but to be heard and to have an immediate impact upon the listeners. This implies, of necessity, that it will have certain characteristics which are not found and are not desirable in written studies.[7]

In naming some of the benefits of expository preaching even, Lloyd-Jones demonstrated a level of receiver/congregation sensitivity. The preacher's goals of variety and a certain kind of ethos[8] are met by expository preaching. His eye was on the congregation when he suggested the goal of variety:

> If there were no other argument for expository preaching this, to me, would be sufficient in and of itself; it will preserve and guarantee variety and variation in your preaching. It will save you from repetition; and that will be a good thing for your people as well as for yourself.[9]

---

5. Ibid., pp. 121, 122.
6. Ibid., pp. 122, 123.
7. Martyn Lloyd-Jones, *Studies in the Sermon on the Mount*, 2 vols. (Grand Rapids: Eerdmans, 1960), 1:vii. Lloyd-Jones quoted Jonathan Edwards in endorsement of his view of the main benefit of the sermon. He said that the main benefit, contrary to objections on the frequency of preaching, is by the " 'impression made upon the mind at the time, and not by the effect that arises afterwards by a remembrance of what was delivered. . . . The memory profits, as it renews and increases that impression.' " "Preaching," in *Anglican and Puritan Thinking* (Rushden: Westminster Conference, 1977), p. 112.
8. Cf. James C. McCroskey's definition of ethos: "The attitude toward a source of a communication held at a given time by a receiver." *Rhetorical*, pp. 71-79. Cf. his treatment and findings on initial, derived, and terminal ethos and the determining factors of each. Ibid. Cf. also Kenneth E. Anderson and Theodore Clevenger, "A Summary of Experimental Research in Ethos," in *Speech Communication: Analysis and Readings*, ed. Howard M. Martin and Kenneth E. Anderson (Boston: Allyn and Bacon, Inc., 1968), pp. 177-200.
9. Lloyd-Jones, *Preaching*, p. 75.

The goal of variety is receiver-centered.

Receiver-centeredness is evident also in Lloyd-Jones's suggestion for the establishment and maintenance of a certain element of the preacher's ethos, the perception of the congregation of him as an interpreter of the Bible:

> So you must be expository; and in any case my whole argument is that it should be clear to people that what we are saying is something that comes out of the Bible. We are presenting the Bible and its message.[10]

Views of Audience Analysis

Secondly, one may examine Lloyd-Jones's statements which reflect his views on audience analysis. He gave as the scriptural basis for audience analysis I Corinthians 3 and Hebrews 5:11ff. This matter of audience analysis seemed to be a kind of axiom with him. He wanted to "emphasize" that the preacher "has to assess the condition of those in the pew" and "to bear that in mind in the preparation and delivery of his message." Again, he did *not* suggest that the listener "is to control." He spoke of the fundamental nature of this exercise:

> The first thing a teacher in any realm has to do is to assess the capacity of his hearers, his pupils, his students, whatever they are. This fundamental rule should be constantly in the mind of the preacher and we need to be reminded of it constantly. . . .[11]

Lloyd-Jones went on to give a warning concerning the care and goal of accuracy in which this exercise is undertaken. He warned that the preacher "must be careful" that this is "a true assessment and an accurate one." He gave an illustration. A main danger, for example, that the preacher faces is "to assume" that all "who claim to be Christians," "who think" they are Christians, and "who are members of the Church," are "therefore of necessity Christians." He called this the "commonest" and "most fatal blunder of all." He saw that this would lead the preacher wrongly to preach always "in a manner suited to Christian believers." He believed that this false

---

10. Ibid. Cf. McCroskey, *Rhetorical,* pp. 71-79, 192; cf. also Abbey, *Communication in Pulpit and Parish* (Philadelphia: Westminster Press, 1973), pp. 92, 96.

11. Ibid., pp. 143, 44. Cf. Jay E. Adams, who also spoke on the fundamental necessity of audience analysis: "Careful analysis of the audience seems to be of prime importance today. Paul *knew* his people. In Antioch and before the Sanhedrin, he was conscious of the factions. He knew Felix well enough to trust to simple exposition. He had taken Agrippa's measure, and made the supreme bid for his soul. He trapped the Athenians at their own game, and commanded their respect. Conservatives today too frequently are found fighting yesterday's battles, building straw men, and employing outmoded modes of adaptation. They often preach to faces, not to well-known and thoroughly understood persons. Paul's preaching loudly proclaims to us that there is a need for better analysis." *Studies in Preaching,* vol. 1: *Audience Adaptations in the Sermons and Speeches of Paul* (Phillipsburg, N.J.: Presbyterian and Reformed, 1976), pp. 68, 69. Lloyd-Jones observed: "A chief fault of the young preacher is to preach to the people as he would like them to be, instead of as they are." *Preaching,* p. 144.

assumption arises from the fact that many people have accepted "the teachings of the Scriptures intellectually," but they "have never come under the power of the Word." He concluded that because they have "never really come under its power," therefore, "they have never truly repented."[12]

A practical result of such audience analysis and awareness on the part of Lloyd-Jones was a rule which he laid down. He urged that there "should always be" one "evangelistic service" in connection with "each church every week." Without "any hesitation," he made this an "absolute rule."[13]

Rudimentary Factors of Message Delivery

Thirdly, one turns to survey Lloyd-Jones's views of message delivery in the light of some rudimentary factors of receiver/congregation awareness. As might be expected from one who achieved wide popularity as a preacher, he has some advice to share concerning this matter of message delivery. Characteristically, he was reluctant to lay down rules. Yet in the actual delivery of sermons, the preacher "must be wrong" in reading his sermon. He recalled that some men in the history of preaching have done so and have been "greatly blessed." But his point was that "you do not make rules out of exceptions."[14]

Lloyd-Jones went on to give an analysis revealing preacher-congregation communication as a process and isolating a chief factor in it for the preacher/communicator/source. This may be seen in his rationale on the above position. He found that there is an *interaction* between the preacher/source and the congregation/receiver. He observed that preaching "involves" a "direct contact between the people and the preacher" and an "interplay of personalities and minds and hearts." He discovered an "element of 'give and take' " in the act of preaching. It is "good," therefore, that the preacher "be looking at the people." He could not accept that a preacher could be "looking at the people and reading a manuscript at the same time." He concluded that such reading caused the preacher to "lose [the congregation's]

---

12. Ibid., pp. 146-50. Cf. Abbey's similar warnings requiring accuracy, lest the effectiveness of the sermon be dulled, *Pulpit*, p. 52. Concerning Jonathan Edwards, Lloyd-Jones said: "The most astonishing thing about this phenomenon, this mighty intellect, was that no man knew more about the workings of the human heart, regenerate or unregenerate, than Jonathan Edwards. If you want to know anything about the psychology of religion, conversion, revivals, read Jonathan Edwards." "Jonathan Edwards and the Crucial Importance of Revival," in *The Puritan Experiment in the New World* (Rushden: Westminster Conference, 1976), p. 133.

13. Ibid., p. 151. Concerning George Whitefield as an evangelist, Lloyd-Jones observed: "One of his great themes was Original Sin. No man could expose the condition of the natural unregenerate heart more powerfully than George Whitefield." "John Calvin and George Whitefield," in *Able Ministers of the New Testament* (London: Puritan and Reformed Studies Conference, 1964, p. 90).

14. Ibid., p. 226. Lloyd-Jones seems to indicate an understanding of McCroskey's conviction that a great part of the communicator's meaning can be stimulated by the delivery of the verbal message. McCroskey, *Rhetorical*, pp. 242, 243.

attention and [his] grip on them," and "[the congregation loses its] grip [on the preacher] and what he [is] saying." A statement by him which reflects his view of the nature of the act of preaching as a communications process is relevant here:

> Surely, by definition, preaching is speech addressed to people in a direct and personal manner. It is not something theoretical or an academic lecture; it implies a living contact. Anything that makes you lose that is bad in and of itself.[15]

The chief factor which assists the preacher-communicator-source in this area, according to Lloyd-Jones is freedom. He saw freedom in the pulpit as the "great thing" which he could not "over-emphasize." He believed this freedom "is of the very essence of the act of preaching."[16] Such is his obvious awareness of the *receiver* and the *channel* in this communication process and message delivery labeled expository preaching.

Summary

In this examination, there has been a rehearsal of some of the general principles and presuppositions of the communications process as discovered and set forth by the science of modern communications. One has surveyed Lloyd-Jones's receiver-centered statements and found that he seemed *unconsciously* to have thought and operated within their confines. As well as having much to say about the *source* and *message* of expository preaching, the prepared expository preacher and his sermon, he also demonstrated a concern for, and an awareness of, the *receiver* and the *channel*. He showed an interest in the *fundamental necessity* of audience awareness and analysis. He was keenly aware of the dynamics which operate in the act of preaching or message delivery. He knew that there was an interaction process, or living contact, which took place. Finally, he believed that whatever might interrupt that process is to be shunned as a distraction.

Conclusion

It may be thus observed that Lloyd-Jones's recommendations in regard to the listeners to preaching seem to be consistent with the basis findings of modern communications research. His theory is now seen to embrace an extra dimension. It is comprehensive. Noting again Lloyd-Jones's success with it, it may be said to be

---

15. Ibid., pp. 227, 228. Cf. the following: McCroskey, who said that a good oral communicator must "take care that his style is also oral rather than written." *Rhetorical*, p. 192; if he uses a manuscript or notes of any kind, he should "write as if (he) were speaking and then read as if (he) had not written." Abbey, *Pulpit*, p. 208; the "wise practice" of physical skills, such as eye contact, is also necessary. Abbey, *Pulpit*, p. 207; this is necessary because the source has as his aim to "interact" with the receiver. Abbey, *Pulpit*, p. 24.

16. Ibid., p. 229.

practical. His insights concerning the audience congregation, therefore, deserve to be considered seriously. These may be part of the secret of his success.

As preachers in the Reformed tradition also, What is our level of audience awareness? Are we correct in continuing that level? Do we engage in audience analysis? Are we keenly aware of these rudimentary factors of message delivery? May we as Reformed pastors today maintain adequate sensitivity in these areas as we proclaim the Christ of the Scriptures. [17]

17. This article was adapted from Robert Lee Penny, ''An Examination of the Principles of Expository Preaching of David Martyn Lloyd-Jones'' (D.Min. thesis, Harding University Graduate School of Religion, 1980), pp. 114-24.

Martin Lloyd-Jones
On the Delivery of Sermons

ROBERT PENNY

Introductory

One of the two irreducible elements of true preaching, according to Lloyd-Jones is the *delivery* or what he would reserve for the strict use of the word "preaching." To him, the preparation of the sermon as a true entity is only the "first half" of the process. The "act of preaching" must be emphasized equally.[1]

Two Provisions

Once we have clearly noted the high premium which Lloyd-Jones placed on the delivery, we can go on to survey the ingredients which, according to him, make up the true act of preaching. Before this, two provisions he laid down concerning the actual delivery of the sermon should also be noted. First, he had a conviction concerning its *unpredictableness*. He held that although the sermon may be ready and there exists confidence in regard to its quality, "you never know what is going to happen when you start preaching, if it's preaching worthy of the name." Second, he maintained a certain *indefinability*. He said that this element is "something difficult to define." He saw it not only as a mistake but harmful to "regard it as a matter of instructions, and rule and regulations, of dos and don'ts." He believed that instead preaching "is something that one recognizes when one hears it," and the "best thing we can do is to say certain things about it." Having seen these two provisions, we may consider the twelve ingredients which Lloyd-Jones listed as necessary to the act of preaching.[2]

---

1. Martyn Lloyd-Jones, *Preaching and Preachers* (Grand Rapids: Zondervan, 1972), p. 80. Of George Whitefield's delivery, Lloyd-Jones said: "I have said something about the man, I have said something about the message, I end with what was the most characteristic thing of all about this man, namely, his preaching. Do you recognize that distinction and division? . . . There is a tremendous difference between uttering truths and preaching." "John Calvin and George Whitefield," in *Able Ministers of the New Testament* (London: Puritan and Reformed Studies Conference, 1964), p. 91.

2. Ibid., pp. 80, 81.

Twelve Ingredients

Involvement of Whole Personality

Lloyd-Jones saw as the first ingredient of authentic preaching the involvement of the whole personality of the preacher. He stated his acceptance of the well-known definition of preaching given by Phillips Brookes that preaching is "truth mediated through personality." Lloyd-Jones's version of the same was put in this way: "In preaching all one's faculties should be engaged, the whole man should be involved."[3]

Sense of Authority

The second ingredient listed by Lloyd-Jones as necessary to the act of preaching is "a sense of authority and control over the congregation and the proceedings." He believed that a distraction occurs when a preacher is "apologetic" or in any way gives the impression that he is speaking only at the permission of the congregation. Neither should he appear to be "tentatively putting forward certain suggestions and ideas." Instead, the idea of a confidence of authority should be promoted.[4]

Freedom

A third indispensable ingredient of the delivery is freedom. He claimed to "attach very great importance" to this ingredient. The essence of this point is that the preacher "must not be too tied in his preparation and by it." He admitted to an apparent contradiction: "It may sound contradictory to say 'prepare, and prepare carefully,' and yet 'be free.' " But he explained that a postulate of this is that preaching "should be always under the Spirit." His cardinal conviction, running throughout his treatise, *Preaching,* goes like this, in one of its briefest forms:

> You will find that the Spirit Who has helped you in your preparation may now help you, while you are speaking, in an entirely new way, and open things out to you which you had not seen while you were preparing your sermon.[5]

He saw this as a major factor promoting freedom while preaching.

Interaction

Lloyd-Jones stated the value of a fourth and often unnoticed ingredient in true preaching which he called the "element of exchange." This exchange or interaction takes place as the preacher "while speaking" is "in a sense" actually "deriving something from his congregation." The second source or party in this exchange is

---

3. Ibid., p. 82. Cf. Abbey's similar conviction about the whole man coming to expression in the delivery. Merrill Abbey, *Communication in Pulpit and Parish* (Philadelphia: Westminster Press, 1973), p. 200.

4. Ibid.

5. Ibid., pp. 83, 85.

"those present in the congregation who are spiritually minded people," and they function to "make their contribution to the occasion."[6]

Seriousness

A fifth ingredient is that of seriousness. Lloyd-Jones held that the preacher "must be" a serious man. He must never allow the idea that preaching is something "light or superficial or trivial." The preacher, on the other hand, must seek to give the impression that "he is dealing with the most serious matter that men and women can ever consider together."[7]

Liveliness

Liveliness is a sixth ingredient, which modifies the fifth and "underlines the fact that seriousness does not mean solemnity, does not mean sadness, [and] does not mean morbidity." Lloyd-Jones maintained that a preacher "must be lively" and that he "can be lively and serious at the same time." This ingredient may be expected to drive out dullness and heaviness.[8]

Zeal

By this next ingredient, zeal, Lloyd-Jones meant generally a "sense of concern." While he acknowledged that these ingredients are "intimately related," he saw a distinct necessity for the preacher to convey always "the impression that he himself has been gripped by what he is saying." The preacher must impress the people that he is "taken up" and "absorbed by what he is doing." He is unmistakably "full of matter," and he is "anxious to impart this." He is "so moved and thrilled" by what he has to communicate "that he wants to share in this." Lloyd-Jones concluded that if the preacher "has not been gripped nobody else will be," so this is "absolutely essential."[9]

---

6. Ibid., p. 84.
7. Ibid., pp. 85, 86.
8. Ibid., p. 87. Lloyd-Jones said that the business of a professor similarly is "to put that on fire, to enthuse, to stimulate, to enliven. And that is the primary business of preaching. Let us take this to heart. Jonathan Edwards laid great emphasis upon this; and what we need above everything else today is moving, passionate, powerful preaching." "Jonathan Edwards and the Crucial Importance of Revival" in *The Puritan Experiment in the New World* (Rushden: Westminster Conference, 1976), p. 112.
9. Ibid., pp. 87, 88. Lloyd-Jones said: "You can preach mechanically, you can preach coldly. . . ." "Sandemanianism," in *Profitable for Doctrine and Reproof* (Foxton: Puritan and Reformed Studies Conference, 1967), pp. 67, 68. Lloyd-Jones gave an example of zeal; he said: "But the thing that characterized the preaching [of George Whitefield] was the zeal, the fire, the passion, the flame. He was a most convincing and alarming preacher." "John Calvin and George Whitefield," p. 92.

Warmth

This takes one almost imperceptibly into the eighth ingredient, warmth. Lloyd-Jones chose, for the sake of contrast, the word "clinical" as the opposite of this virtue. He saw that sometimes all the preacher's actions are "almost perfect," but the result is coldness. He claimed that it is not "moving" because "the man has not been moved himself." He believed that "should never be true of the preacher."[10]

Urgency

Lloyd-Jones also listed urgency as an indispensable ingredient of true preaching. He admitted the kinship of this ingredient with others but believed that it ought to be "isolated and underlined in and of itself." He saw this as the thing that "makes preaching such an astonishing act and such a responsible and overwhelming matter."[11]

Persuasiveness

The tenth ingredient is persuasiveness. This is the "whole object of this act." The preacher does not "say things with the attitude of 'take it or leave it.' " His desire should be to persuade people of the truth. He is not "giving a learned disquisition on a text" or a "display of his own knowledge." Lloyd-Jones maintained that the preacher must remember that "he is dealing with living souls" and that he "wants to move them, to take them with him, [and] to lead them to the Truth."[12]

Pathos

The eleventh ingredient listed by Lloyd-Jones as indispensable to authentic preaching is quite distinctive. He called it pathos. It is related to a love for the people to whom one preaches and is the offspring of compassion. He pointed to the Lord as one

---

10. Ibid., p. 89. Lloyd-Jones commented on George Whitefield's observation of what occurred when Whitefield preached to the coal miners of Kingswood: "Whitefield says, 'As I was preaching to them I suddenly began to observe white furrows in their black faces.' What was it? Oh, the tears were streaming down their faces and making furrows in the coal dust and grime. That is preaching!" "John Calvin and George Whitefield," p. 92.

11. Ibid., p. 92. Cf. the idea of Raymond McLaughlin that an effective communicator has an urgency and a desire to communicate. *Communication For The Church* (Grand Rapids: Zondervan, 1968), p. 194. Lloyd-Jones found an example in Howell Harris, a Welsh preacher: "This is the only explanation of this man. This is what created within him a compassion for the lost. This is what urged him to go out and tell the people about their condition and to do something about them. His concern for the lost and perishing was the consuming passion of his soul." "Howell Harris and Revival," in *Adding to the Church* (Foxton: The Westminster Conference, 1973), p. 74.

12. Ibid., p. 92. Lloyd-Jones spoke critically of preachers who followed a mere intellectual approach: "All you have to do is believe and accept the teaching of the Church. You accept that with your mind and that is all that is necessary." "Sandemanianism," p. 58.

who saw the multitudes as sheep without a shepherd and had compassion on them. He maintained that "if you know nothing of this you should not be in the pulpit, for this is certain to come out in your preaching." The second parent of this offspring is the "matter itself" which the preacher seeks to communicate. He highlighted an illustration of this ingredient when he related how a great actor of the eighteenth century, David Garrick, wished that he could utter the word "Mesopotamia" as George Whitefield could and said that he would give a hundred guineas if he coud but utter the word "Oh!" with Whitefield's same pathos. Lloyd-Jones believed that Whitefield's preaching, because of the love of God in his heart, had this "melting quality."[13]

In order to clarify and to balanced these expressions by Lloyd-Jones, the contrast drawn between emotion and emotionalism should be seen. To explain his distaste for the latter, he said there is to him "nothing more hateful than a man who deliberately tries to play on the surface and superficial emotions of people." But he held the conviction that if a man is not "moved" by the truth, he "does not belong to that company, that category which includes the great Apostle himself." He gave as an example of the emotion of the apostle Paul the "sheer grand emotion" of the conclusion to Romans 11. Fearful of overreaction against excesses and emotionalism, Lloyd-Jones stated that the truth itself may be in jeopardy unless we find the healthy balance. He said:

> The Gospel of Jesus Christ takes up the whole man, and if what purports to be the Gospel does not do so it is not the Gospel. The Gospel is meant to do that, and does that. The whole man is involved because the Gospel leads to regeneration; and so I say that this element of pathos and emotion, this element of being moved, should always be prominent in our preaching.[14]

Power

The final ingredient of true preaching, according to Lloyd-Jones is power. By this he meant the "influence" or assistance of the Holy Spirit. He made reference again to Paul's statement in I Corinthians 2:4 concerning preaching "in demonstration of the Spirit and of power." He also cited I Thessalonians 1:5 as a reference to this ingredient: "Our gospel came not unto you in word only, but also in power, and in the Holy Ghost, and in much assurance." His observation was this: "True preaching, after all, is God acting. It is not just a man uttering words; it is God using him. . . ."[15]

---

13. Ibid., pp. 92, 93. Lloyd-Jones explained the effects of pathos in the preaching of Whitefield; it had "a love and melting quality that were irresistible." "John Calvin and George Whitefield," p. 92.

14. Ibid., pp. 94, 95. Cf. McLaughlin's condemnation of "pulpit oratory divorced from love." *Communication*, p. 200.

15. Ibid., p. 95. Lloyd-Jones again gave as his illustration Whitefield, and he gave a

Reflections: An Illustration

It seems important now to survey Lloyd-Jones's statement of summary regarding these two irreducible elements of preaching, the sermon and the act of preaching. He said that they must be "combined in their right proportions" and that "both must be emphasized." He gave an illustration of the interdependence of the two. Although told in the third person, the story apparently related one of his own experiences. He told how a preacher might take a sermon which seemed to have effectiveness in his own congregation and seek to preach that same sermon to another congregation. But once the preacher has begun to preach that sermon, he suddenly finds that he has "got virtually nothing" and it "all seems to collapse" in his hands. To make this point, Lloyd-Jones asks the question concerning the differnce between the two occasions. He gave this observation:

> What happened on the previous Sunday when you were preaching that sermon in your own pulpit was that the Spirit came upon you, or perhaps upon the people, (it may well have been, as I have previously explained, that it was mainly the people, and you received it from them) and your little sermon was taken up, and you were given this special function and authority in an unusual manner, and so you had that exceptional service. But you are in different circumstances with a different congregation and you yourself may be feeling different. So you now have to rely upon your sermon; and you suddenly find that you haven't much of a sermon.[16]

Table 1

Martin Lloyd-Jones's
12 Ingredients of Delivery ("Preaching")

1. Involvement of whole personality/whole man
2. Sense of authority/confidence/control over proceedings
3. Freedom/not tied to preparation
4. Interaction with congregation/element of exchange
5. Seriousness/most serious subject ever/eternal destinies at stake
6. Liveliness/not sad
7. Zeal/sense of concern/gripped
8. Warmth/not clinical/cold

---

warning to those of Calvinistic persuasion: "The danger of those who follow the teaching of Calvin . . . is that they tend to become intellectualists, or they tend to sink in what I would describe as an 'ossified orthodoxy.' And that is of no value, my friends. You need the power of the Spirit upon it. To state the Truth is not enough, it must be stated 'in demonstration of the Spirit and of power.' And that is what this mighty man so gloriously illustrates." "John Calvin and George Whitefield," p. 95.

16. Ibid., p. 96.

9. Urgency/overwhelming matter to be considered
10. Persuasiveness/not take it or leave it approach
11. Pathos/offspring of compassion/emotion
12. Power/assistance/influence of the Holy Spirit

Here one can see how Lloyd-Jones isolated these two elements in actual practice. He saw clear difference between having a sermon, however well-prepared and excellent, and the ultimate effectiveness of it at the conclusion of the act of preaching. Even Lloyd-Jones seems to have been made painfully aware of this distinction. He called this "a great mystery," and he gave a brief word of advice: "You must not rely on either the one or the other. You must not rely on your sermon only, you must not rely on the preaching only; both are essential to true preaching."[17]

Recapitulation

A recapitulation seems in order. We have seen the initial *two provisions* Lloyd-Jones laid down concerning the act of preaching or the delivery, *unpredictableness* and *indefinability*. Following upon the latter, we saw how he would venture to give *ingredients only* of what he observed to be authentic preaching. Then we saw how carefully he *isolated* this element of the delivery from the preparation of the sermon itself. One of his last words on the matter is the word "mystery." It seems, therefore, that one is left at a point of tension and can pursue the matter no further. No approach, however scientific, can search out the limits of that which is admittedly mysterious. Lloyd-Jones seems to desire to go no further.

Conclusion

To Lloyd-Jones, then, there must be both elements: the sermon and the delivery. Effective expository preaching is a combination of *both*. It would seem, therefore, that Lloyd-Jones would teach that the developing preacher must seek to *major* in *both*.

Could this be part of Lloyd-Jones's secret? Clearly, he had a firm grasp on both elements. This concept of equal importance should serve as a stimulus and regulator for any expository preacher.[18]

---

17. Ibid., pp. 96, 97.
18. This article was adapted from Robert Lee Penny, "An Examination of the Principles of Expository Preaching of David Martyn Lloyd-Jones" (D.Min. thesis, Harding University Graduate School of Religion, 1980), pp. 79-90.

A Suggestion For
Young Preachers—

AND SOME OLDER ONES TOO!

Recently listening to a young man who has great promise preach, I was reminded afresh of a fact of which I became aware early in my teaching of homiletics at Westminster Theological Seminary:

YOUNG PREACHERS—AND SOME OLDER ONES TOO—TEND TO PREACH TOO MUCH IN A SERMON.

The sermon to which I refer ranged far and wide, over Old Testament and New, into various doctrines and their subpoints, all (mind you) in 25 minutes! Apparently, the young man had never considered the fact that *you can say more about less*.

Were I to attempt to describe the activities in which I was engaged last summer in 25 minutes, I'd be saying such things as

Then I went to several other places (I wish I had time to tell you where and all about them) and did some very interesting things (perhaps at some later time I could mention these in detail), etc., etc.

But, if I took 25 minutes to tell you about one event on one night at one place last summer, I could tell all—colorfully, interestingly, and in a way that you could understand. Instead of hurriedly racing hither and yon, I could stop, examine in detail, describe in depth, delineate and delete! But all of last summer? Why all I could do is vaguely sketch what took place!

The same is true of preaching. The young man had a decently chosen preaching portion, but, instead of delving into it, he ran all over the Bible. He should have explored its main *telos* (purpose) in depth, related it carefully to the contemporary scene, and sent us away with one whale of an impact from the Word of God. Instead, we went out barely touched by it. His effort was dissipated by scattering his shot. Someone has said, "A rifle is more powerful than a shotgun."

So, let's stop using buckshot in the pulpit.

Now, for my suggestion. Preachers are always looking for ways to reuse old sermons. That is OK; New Testament preachers did. But here is one of the best ways of all. Review your first three to five years' sermons. You will notice that (if you are like most novices) you tried to preach the entire corpus of Christian truth in every message.

"OK," you say, "I've looked at them (shudder!), and the charge is true. What do I do now?" My suggestion is this:

Use each of the three to five points in each sermon, itself as the basis for a complete sermon. Perhaps some points could be so fully elaborated (remember, you can say more about less) that they could form the basis for a series of sermons.

There, you have it. Take it to heart. Don't dump those old, unusable sermons in the wastebasket. There is some valuable ore there to be mined. Go to it, now that you know how!—J.E.A.

Don't Tell Us What You Are Going to Do—Do It

I have been noting a tendency among preachers that is common enough to warrant a label; I have called it *prefacing*. Prefacing is the bad habit of announcing what one is about to do before doing it, *when there is no reason for doing so* (note the important italicized qualification).

Let me suggest two ways in which prefacing frequently takes place in preaching:

1. When one announces beforehand the points in his sermon;
2. When he announces beforehand that he is about to illustrate.

An example of the first is exactly what I did in the last paragraph. Reread it and you will discover what I am talking about. And to go on to illustrate the second point I could now say, "Let me give you an example of what I am talking about" (of course, as you see, I just did).

But what is wrong with prefacing? When there is no good reason to do so, it breaks the continuity of what one has been saying by calling attention away from the content to the structure by which that content is being presented.

Foolishly, some homileticians have declared that a preacher should announce all of the points in every sermon. Why? Because they said so, that's why. There is no other good reason. No biblical precedent for doing so can be found. Search the Scriptures and you will not find a single instance of anyone announcing, "This morning I should like to tell you three facts about hell" (or whatever). It just doesn't happen. It doesn't happen because it *shouldn't* happen. Such prefacing adds nothing and certainly detracts.

Now, I did mention a qualification. One *should* announce points if, and *only* if, by doing so he furthers content. That is to say, if, for instance, there are "two steps and only two steps" in dealing with a habit pattern (putting off/putting on), and it is important to stress that there are no more and no less, then the steps and their number become a part of the content itself.

That is the *only* time when it is right to announce points: when knowing the points themselves in some way contributes to the discussion. Otherwise, prefacing and announcing distracts.

Again, the same principle holds true for announcing the use of examples and illustrations. It is always wrong to do so unless it serves a better purpose than buying time for the speaker to think (that should have been done before entering the pulpit). There *are* times, of course, when calling attention to the fact that one is about to use an example can be useful. Consider this: ''The example I am about to use does not *always* apply, nor does it apply to *everyone*. As you listen, then, ask yourself, is this for me?'' In a case like this, where it is important for the listener to evaluate what he is about to hear in a certain way, prefacing the example can be useful—indeed, vital.

But most prefacing—of examples, of points in a sermon, of biblical passages about to be read—is filler. One of the things that makes sermons dull and uninviting is filler.

So, from now on let me give you this word of advice. Stop telling us what you are going to do—just do it. Don't announce points, just make them; don't preface examples, just give them—and your sermons will be smoother and more powerful as a result.—J.E.A.

Hebrew Helps
for
Busy Pastors

MILTON FISHER
In collaboration with
DWIGHT ZELLER

Milton Fisher is professor of Old Testament at the Reformed Episcopal Seminary, Philadelphia. He was formerly director of the Cooperative Language Institute, Addis Ababa, Ethiopia.

Dwight Zeller is director of Sangre de Cristo School for Biblical Studies, Westcliffe, Colorado. He is formerly professor of Greek, Hebrew, and homiletics at the Reformed Episcopal Seminary.

Introduction to the Sixth
In the Series of
HEBREW HELPS

Lesson 29 picks up with an important Review and Summary, including an absolutely obligatory drill quiz. NEVER TAKE SHORT-CUTS IN YOUR LANGUAGE LEARNING—progress is made only by repetition and review.

Use the worksheet as you were instructed earlier, by laying thin paper over the quiz page and filling in the blanks, which can then be checked for correctness by reference to the facing page. By this procedure, furthermore, the quiz can be repeated immediately or on later occasions—all a part of that vital repetition and review.

Likewise, do not forget to REVIEW EARLIER LESSONS from time to time, reusing also the earlier Review and Summary worksheets. To repeat, in hopes you will remember to repeat, language is *learned* by *repetition,* not by one-time memorization efforts.

LESSON TWENTY-NINE
REVIEW AND SUMMARY OF LESSONS 23-28

Study the chart, then write in proper vowel for the Article form:

Initial letter of noun or adjective	Form of Article
עַ or הַ with UNaccented ָ חַ with ָ , regardless of accent	הֶ
עַ otherwise than above, as well as אַ or רַ	הָ
הַ or חַ with other than the above pointing (Daghesh-forte IMPLIED)	הַ
ALL OTHER letters take the normal form	־הַ·

Study the chart, then write the names of the STEMS and fill in the indicators (vowel points) for the 3 m. sg. Perfect and Imperfect of the STRONG VERB.

	SIMPLE	INTENSIVE	CAUSATIVE
A C T I V E	**QAL** Pf. כָּתַב Impf. יִכְתֹּב	**PIEL** כִּתֵּב יְכַתֵּב	**HIPHIL** הִכְתִּיב יַכְתִּיב
P A S S I V E	**NIPHAL** Pf. נִכְתַּב Impf. יִכָּתֵב	**PUAL** כֻּתַּב יְכֻתַּב	**HOPHAL** הָכְתַּב יָכְתַּב
R E C I P.		**HITHPAEL** Pf. הִתְכַּתֵּב Impf. יִתְכַּתֵּב	

LESSON TWENTY-NINE
Review and Summary of Lessons 23-28 (WORKSHEET)

Study the chart, then write in proper vowel for the Article form:

Initial letter of noun or adjective	Form of Article
ע or ה with UNaccented ָ ח with ָ , regardless of accent	הַ
ע otherwise than above, as well as א or ר	הָ
ה or ח with other than the above pointing (Daghesh-forte IMPLIED)	הֶ
ALL OTHER letters take the normal form	הַ

Study the chart, then write the names of the STEMS and fill in the indicators (vowel points) for the 3 m. sg. Perfect and Imperfect of the STRONG VERB.

	SIMPLE	INTENSIVE	CAUSATIVE
A C T I V E	Pf. כתב Impf. כתב	כתב כתב	כת ב כת ב
P A S S I V E	Pf. כתב Impf. כתב	כתב כתב	כתב כתב
R E C I P.		Pf. כתב Impf. כתב	

LESSON TWENTY-NINE (continued)
Review and Summary of Lessons 23-28

Add the **Imperfect** WAW-CONSECUTIVE indicator and the vowel point-ing for: וַיֹּאמֶר

The **Perfect** WAW-CONSECUTIVE is written the same as the simple con-junction; therefore only the __CONTEXT__ indicates the difference.

In Lamedh-He weak verbs with pronominal suffix, as אֶרְאֶךָ and וְאֶעֱשֶׂךָ (objects) and עָשׂוּ (subject), the ה __DISAPPEARS__.

In PIEL of a strong verb type, the middle consonant doubles, but if that middle letter is a Guttural (including Resh), as in אֲבָרֶכְךָ, the consonant __REJECTS__ the doubling, and by way of compensation the preceding vowel is __HEIGHTENED__ (or, lengthened).

An initial letter מ- often (in stems Piel, Pual, Hithpael, Hiphil and Hophal) indicates the word is a __PARTICIPLE__, as מְבָרְכֶיךָ.

There are two very common verbs which "misbehave"— וַיֵּלֶךְ or לָלֶכֶת behaves as though it had a __PE-YODH__ type weakness, al-though its Root form is הָלַךְ.

וַיִּקַּח behaves as though it had a __PE-NUN__ weakness, although the Root form is לָקַח.

בְּ ("in, at" = "when") or לְ ("to"), when prefixed onto forms like בְּצֵאתוֹ and לָלֶכֶת show that they are verbs in the form of __INFINITIVE__ __CONSTRUCT__.

The initial Nun in נָתַן often __ASSIMILATES__ into (or, with) the תּ, so that in consequence the תּ is __DOUBLED__. As a result, the first person QAL IMPERFECT form is אֶתֵּן.

120

LESSON TWENTY-NINE (continued)
Review and Summary of Lessons 23-28 (WORKSHEET)

Add the **Imperfect** WAW-CONSECUTIVE indicator and the vowel pointing for: וַיּאׁמֶר

The **Perfect** WAW-CONSECUTIVE is written the same as the simple conjunction; therefore only the _____ indicates the difference.

In Lamedh-He weak verbs with pronominal suffix, as אַרְאֶךָ and וְאֶעֱשְׂךָ (objects) and עָשׂוּ (subject), the ה _____.

In PIEL of a strong verb type, the middle consonant doubles, but if that middle letter is a Guttural (including Resh), as in אֲבָרֶכְךָ , the consonant _____ the doubling, and by way of compensation the preceding vowel is _____ (or, lengthened).

An initial letter מ- often (in stems Piel, Pual, Hithpael, Hiphil and Hophal) indicates the word is a _____, as מְבָרְכֶיךָ .

There are two very common verbs which "misbehave"— וַיֵּלֶךְ or לָלֶכֶת behaves as though it had a _____ type weakness, although its Root form is

וַיִּקַּח behaves as though it had a _____ weakness, although the Root form is

בְּ ("in, at" = "when") or לְ ("to"), when prefixed onto forms like בְּצֵאתוֹ and לָלֶכֶת show that they are verbs in the form of

_____ _____.

The initial Nun in נָתַן often _____ into (or, with) the ת , so that in consequence the ת is _____. As a result, the first person QAL IMPERFECT form is אֶתֵּן .

121

LESSON THIRTY
WEAK VERBS — A STRONG SHOWING!

Turn in your own Hebrew text to the first chapter of Jonah. Read through the first five verses for a quick impression as to the TYPES of verbs which occur there—strong (normal) and weak verbs. Do it *now*, then return to this lesson material.

The *first* surprise should be the great number of verbs you found—twenty-five verbs in just five verses. The *second* jolt comes when a comparative count is made between the strong (two) and weak (twenty-three!) verb TYPES.

Such a predominance of WEAK VERBS, the vast-majority role they play in general usage, may at first seem threatening to the student. Relax, please, and calmly consider two facts: (1) We can only take a language *as it comes,* and conclude that it is necessary to apply ourselves to the study of kinds and behavior patterns of the weak verbs types (a limited number of classes); and, somewhat encouraging, (2) the very frequency of the weak verbs' occurrence means that if we read Hebrew with regularity, we can and will become familiar with these constantly recurring forms.

Let's now examine that verb count together, identifying TYPES.

Verse One—Strong: Zero

    Weak: וַיְהִי Middle-weak (or Hollow) and Lamedh-He

           לֵאמֹר Pe-Aleph

Verse Two—Strong: Zero

    Weak: קוּם Middle-weak (Hollow, or Ayin-Waw)

           לֵךְ Root (הָלַךְ) behaves like a Pe-Yodh

           וּקְרָא Lamedh-Aleph and Ayin-Guttural

           עָלְתָה Pe-Guttural and Lamedh-He

Verse Three—Strong: Zero

    Weak: וַיָּקָם Middle-weak (Hollow, or Ayin-Waw)

LESSON THIRTY (continued)

לִבְרׂחַ   Both Ayin- and Lamedh-Guttural

וַיֵּרֶד   Pe-Yodh (and Resh = Ayin-Guttural)

וַיִּמְצָא   Lamedh-Aleph

בָּאָה   Hollow (Ayin-Waw) and Lamedh-Aleph

וַיִּתֵּן   Pe-Nun

וַיֵּרֶד   (See above)

לָבוֹא   (See above)

Verse Four—Strong: לְהִשָּׁבֵר

     Weak: הֵמִיל   Middle-weak (Hollow, or Ayin-Waw)

וַיְהִי   (See above)

חָשְׁבָה   Pe-Guttural

Verse Five—Strong: וַיִּשְׁכַּב

     Weak: וַיִּירְאוּ   Pe-Yodh, Ayin-Guttural, Lamedh-Aleph

וַיִּזְעָקוּ   Ayin-Guttural

וַיִּמְלְלוּ   (See above)

לְהָקֵל   Double-Ayin

יָרַד   Pe-Yodh, Ayin-Guttural

וַיֵּרָדַם   Pe-Guttural

Note: (1) The types count of two to twenty-three means 92% weak!

       (2) As described above the weak TYPES are over-classified, in the sense that some of the weaknesses named have not actually affected the spelling (sound) *in this particular instance*, although they might do so elsewhere. What is essential is to be able to identify in a given

123

LESSON THIRTY (continued)

form the modification which has been produced by a specific phonetic weakness in that verb.

(3) The reason for sharpening one's skill at IDENTIFYING weak verbs by type is for getting at the spelling of the ROOT, so the verb can be looked up in the lexicon for exegetical information.

Finally, your work assignment for this lesson is to go down the verb list, given above. Examine the forms IN BIBLE VERSE CONTEXT, to determine for yourself (use lexicon, a grammar, even an analytical lexicon, if you really are stuck—and ONLY then) the verb's Aspect (or "tense"— Perfect or Imperfect) or Mood (ptc., infin., imperative?), plus other descriptive particulars—such as Waw-consecutive, personal subjects, stem (Qal, etc.). Fortunately there are no object suffixes to contend with in this particular set of verbs.

LESSON THIRTY-ONE

The approach taken in our immediately preceding lesson was to assemble a random set of weak verbs, taking them AS THEY OCCURRED in a particular passage. We shall now organize this data, filling out the entire range of weak verb types, so as to include the other possibilities.

Remember that this is not to be considered abstract or idealized grammatical analysis, but rather very practical information, essential to the identification FOR RECOGNITION of verb roots to make possible your locating them in your lexicon. In some cases, where a radical is not actually lost, it is still useful to be able to explain a variant spelling (from the strong verb norm), as in the case of vocalic accommodation to the gutturals.

In some cases, as shown in Lesson 30, there are alternate options as to names given the weak verb types. There is also a basic difference in terminology with respect to indication of the three radicals of verb roots. Dr. Thomas O. Lambdin, author of the excellent textbook, *Introduction to Biblical Hebrew* (Scribner's, 1971), simply substitutes for the traditional nomenclature, Pe, Ayin, and Lamed syllables—I, II, III. The former is based on the Hebrew (and Arabic) verb, פָּעַל "do, make."

124

LESSON THIRTY-ONE (continued)

Before actually charting the weak verb TYPES (do remember that key reference word), the following related or alternate terminologies are to be noted, after which by "common consent" we shall settle for one label for each type.

1. Strong Verbs may also be referred to as Sound Triliteral Roots. They contain no phonetically weak ("drop-out") or 'demanding' (guttural sounds demand 'a' vowels) letters to alter the normal pattern or spelling of the personal inflexion paradigms.
2. The Ayin-Waw and Ayin-Yodh (latter is less common than former) are grouped together as a class, called Middle-weak or Hollow Verbs.
3. The Pe-Waw type is, by reason of Hebrew (and other Northwest Semitic) phonology, a sub-category of the Pe-Yodh. (cf. יָלַד "he fathered" with *walad*, in Arabic, Ethiopic, Akkadian.)
4. Double-Ayin ("Ayin-Ayin" to some) can also be named a Geminate Verb, as by Lambdin, since the radicals II and III are twins.

Here is a picture of the entire weak clan, ten varieties, in all:

	ל (III)	ע (II)	פ (I)
1-3	Guttural	Guttural	Guttural
4-5	Aleph		Aleph
6	He		
7			Yodh (/Waw)
8			Nun
9		Hollow	
10	Double - Ayin		

An old (1887) Hebrew manual, by W. H. Lowe, contains a clever little rhyme to serve as a guide for our recognizing of all but the first three (the gutturals) of these verb types. You may or may not like to memorize such a poem, but DO PRACTICE listing for yourself the ten weak verb types, so that you can tell what your options are when you come upon forms which are not standard (strong) ones.

LESSON THIRTY-ONE (continued)
'Rules' for FINDING ROOTS

The *servile* letters cast away,
And if behind *three* letters stay,
You HAVE the *root* without delay.

לחם > וַיִּלָּחֶם

But if you have not letters three,
The root will then *defective* be.

Perhaps you then may find it soon
Under *initial* Yodh, or Nun.

ישׁב > תֵּשֶׁב
נפל > יִפֹּל

A *medial* Vav (= Waw) or Yodh
    may show
The letters three you want to know.

קום > הֲקִימֹ֫תִי

Perhaps the radical that's second
To make the three must *twice*
    be reckoned.

סבב > יְסֻבֶּ֫הוּ

Or, finally, perhaps you may
Require to *add* a final He.

בנה > וַיִּ֫בֶן

(We may add: The *order* of these is mostly good,
      'Cept He somewhat sooner try you should!)

NOTE: This ASSUMES that you do have basic control (at least for a passive recognition in context) of the STRONG VERB inflexions— the two Aspects and the Participle, Infinitive, and Imperative Mood.

    More helpful than learning "rules" for weak verb variations is gaining familiarity with the structural pattern (paradigm) of a high frequency SAMPLE VERB of each type, such as:

build	בָּנָה	לָ"ה
fall	נָפַל	פ"נ
stand, rise	קוּם	Hollow
lie down	יָשַׁב	פ"י
surround	סָבַב	Double -ע
find	מָצָא	לָ"א

126

LESSON THIRTY-TWO

The last two lessons grew out of observations of verb forms, specifically, in the first five verses of the book of the prophet Jonah. If you have done the analysis of those verb forms, as directed, you are a long way into the comprehension of the passage. The verbs of Hebrew go a long way, themselves, in telling the story. Not only the *action* but the *flavor* of Hebrew composition comes through in the verbal constructions. Derived *stems, aspects,* and *moods* all add color and definition to the narrative.

As a first step in this lesson, therefore, read those five verses again, making certain you have a good grasp of the forms and precise meanings of the verbs. Then, take note of the following syntactical features of this passage.

Verse 1. The English "came" gives a stronger or more active sense than the Hebrew idiom, which says, "And/ now the word of Jehovah (CONSTRUCT CHAIN) *was*/ happened to Jonah. . . ." We are informed WHAT occurred, not the manner or means by which the revelation came, except that it was *verbal*—"saying" literally, "to say" (Construct Infinitive).

Compare the use of אֶל־ (*"to* Jonah") in verse one and "to Nineveh" in verse two with the *He-directive* affix in verse three, תַּרְשִׁישָׁה "to/ toward Tarshish."

Verse 3. Here is a good place to recall use of the dot called *Mappiq* in the final-He of a feminine affix—both *possessive* (שְׂכָרָהּ "her hire, fare") and *objective* (בָהּ "into her, it").

לָבוֹא is a *purpose* infinitive, while לֵאמֹר in verse one was the *complementary* usage. Remember, an infinitive of purpose MUST have the preposition prefixed; complementary *may,* but not obligatory.

Verse 4. Hebrew is often highly picturesque in expression; so we read that the ship, literally, "thought to be broken." (The closely related Ugaritic literature speaks of ships "dying" in a storm at sea.) Here also, God "casts" a great wind to (= "upon") the sea.

Verse 5. Of the several words for "man" in Hebrew (check an English concordance which keys in with the Hebrew terms), אִישׁ means "individual"; therefore here *"each* man" cried out to his deity.

Hebrew prepositions often carry an almost verbal 'weight'—which is really where we get the "came" in verse one, implied by *"to* Jonah." Here in verse five, "which in the ship" implies the verb "to be"—hence, "which *was* in the ship." (There are, in fact, to balance what we've said about verbs in Hebrew, frequently occuring *nominal* or non-verbal sentences or clauses in biblical Hebrew. This has been observed in our earlier lessons.) So too, in verse seven of this chapter, (And let us know/ find out) by-which-who this evil to us" = ". . . *has come upon us."*

Can you now understand and explain every word in these verses of the first chapter of Jonah? you have recourse to lexicons and English translations to help identify each word, and if you've moved with us through the former "Hebrew Helps," there should be little mystery left—that a little effort can't clear up.

LESSON THIRTY-THREE

For a fifth and final lesson in this set, you are asked simply to strike out on your own into the succeeding verses in Jonah, chapter 1. Major forms and concepts—verbal, nominal, adjectival, etc.—have been treated in the HELPS so far, so by review-reference and by use of other Hebrew language tools you possess, you should be gaining the skills for comprehending narrative text.

Next time we shall deal with some of the 'niceties' of clause syntax—consecution, interrogatives, conditions, etc., and make some more suggestions about use of lexicons, grammars, and concordances. Then, we can get on into serious exegesis.

Do you have some unsettling problems and unanswered questions which these HEBREW HELPS haven't settled for you? Write to us, care of the JOURNAL OF PASTORAL PRACTICE.

Please address all inquiries to:
Dr. Jay E. Adams, Editor-In-Chief
Christian Counseling and Educational Foundation
1790 East Willow Grove Ave.
Laverock, Pa. 19118

Subscription to this Journal is available.
Please inquire with CCEF at the above address.

ISBN: 0-87552-036-7